(weakside ar)

55 I   Covey 96 HB

split   covey 96 slot option wide

B arr)   55 lead

T.O.)

MBI FIY | YI

heel

TB 55 lead

592 left, 560 left

Pass 6 texas split

SI, CB, curl

Pass 6 (FLANK T.O.)

62, 62 all curl (100K)

70 texas split

SI, CB, curl

86 QUICK BAT

B)

THEY will repeat the sa

84 slot scram

(slot   99

scram)

fly 40

50

split curl

(alert kask of

PBL zone

6-9

same as 3-5

86 zero CBS

86 DBL D

72 HBS O

pass 6 t

split CB, 5

TB 55 lead

70 texas sw

SI, CB, cur

AI 560 left

pass 6 tex

FB arr. T

TEM I

37th, pass

10+

fly 92

split

FI

Euclid Public Library
631 E. 222nd Street
Euclid, Ohio 44123
216-261-5300

Published by Cleveland Landmarks Press, Inc.
14189 Washington Boulevard, University Heights, Ohio 44118
www.clevelandlandmarkspress.com (216) 658 4144
©2017, Cleveland Landmarks Press, Inc.
All Rights Reserved
ISBN: 978-0-936760-00-1
LIBRARY OF CONGRESS NUMBER: 2017950148
Book Design by John Yasenosky, III
Printed by Bookmasters, Ashland, Ohio

Front cover image: photo by Focus on Sport/Getty Images
Back cover image: photo by Daniel Krivenki, Think Media Studios
All other images courtesy of Bernie Kosar's personal sports memorabilia image archive

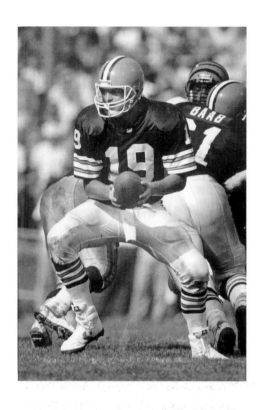

BERNIE KOSAR
LEARNING to SCRAMBLE

BY
BERNIE KOSAR

WITH
CRAIG STOUT

CONTENTS

ACKNOWLEDGMENTS

I have been blessed to have so many positive people in my life. Tons of friends, family members, coaches, teachers, and teammates have made me a better person. Many teammates I played with made me who I am, and words can't do justice to their impact on me as a player and person. Legendary coaches such as Bear Bryant, Howard Schnellenberger, and Don Shula often would say that every day is a new day, and that you never stay the same. You get better or worse every day. I know I'm trying to get better every day, and it's because I have had some incredible people in my life encouraging me along the way. My grade school and high school teachers, and my professors at the University of Miami, especially Drs. Bill Heuson, Andrea Heuson, and Philip Robins, were instrumental in changing my life. In great times and rough times, they, along with too many others to mention, shaped me profoundly and gave me the confidence to strive for my goals. Thank you to all those who influenced me as a child and young man.

When I think of mentors in my life, I think of Schnellenberger, my head coach at the U, who showed unwavering faith in a skinny, awkward kid from Youngstown. He taught me how to be a leader and he trusted my judgment, allowing me to come into my own in college. And then I think of Gary Danielson. He took me under his wing when I entered the NFL, and not only did he help me make the transition to the pros, but he became a close friend to me along the way.

In the last couple of decades, I have a fantastic group of supporters and friends who have been integral to my life. I can't say enough for Brock Milstein and his dad, Carl. Their advice and support of me has made all the difference – they have made me feel like family. Umberto Fedeli has also been like a brother to me, too. He's been in my life for 25 years and has seen my triumphs and tribulations. His beautiful family has become an important part of my life. Tim Hyland, along with our crew, works so much with me throughout Northeast Ohio and has been a huge part of my life in the last few decades. I have developed an excellent friendship with Doug Boojay and his outstanding father Mr. Boojay. Jim Trout has been a great friend and adviser, too. Finally, Nathan Lancry helped enrich my life with this quote, "passion fuels character beyond expectations." I think of that every day, so thank you, Nathan. Of course, thank you to my University of Miami family, especially those who were or continue to be a part of the institution and the Board. People like current Board chair Richard Fain and past chair Stuart Miller, along with all my brothers and sisters from the U, have reinforced my strong belief in the importance of friends and family. Jim Allen and the Seminole tribe in Florida have shown themselves to be true friends who have stuck with me through the tough times. You find your best friends in bad times, not good ones. My appreciation also extends to Don Washkewicz, who has always been a source of knowledge for keeping me healthy and introducing me to incredible doctors. Finally, a heartfelt thank you to Stewart Kohl, who has inspired me with his business guidance and his deep, genuine love of Cleveland.

As far as this book is concerned, I can't express my appreciation enough for Joe LoConti and Dan Clark who encouraged me to get my ideas and stories on paper. They are friends and brothers to me. Thanks, too, to Craig Stout, who spent countless hours with me crafting the book and hearing me tell far more stories than ever made it in the book. I also appreciate all the hard work and expertise from the folks at Think Media. Finally, I'd like to thank Marty Mason for connecting me to Cleveland Landmarks Press and all their people. Thanks to Peter Harvan, who spent a tremendous amount of time editing the manuscript and getting the words just right. Thanks, too, to Jinle Zhu for editing the manuscript. John Yasenosky, expertly designed the book with creativity and professionalism. Finally, thanks to Greg Deegan for putting it all together.

No thanks would be complete without mentioning the wonderful love and support of my better half, Anna. I love you. Of course, my kids have been everything to me: Sara, Rachel, Rebecca, and Joseph. You make my life complete and I love you so much.

This book is a result of real collaboration. Its strengths are due to the generosity of my helpers. The weaknesses are my own.

Bernie Kosar

Chapter 1
LEARNING to SCRAMBLE

Scramble? Bernie Kosar? If people remember anything about my playing career, I'm sure it's not my scrambling ability. I was as slow and as awkward as professional quarterbacks come. Picture Big Bird in the backfield. But the NFL is not Sesame Street. When I was flushed from the pocket, I had to flee for my life; but more often than not, I wound up planted in the turf, not scampering nimbly around tacklers. So why the title?

Admittedly, I won't be talking about scrambling in the literal sense of running away from trouble – big trouble – 300-pound trouble. Instead, I will focus on how football requires an almost masochistic willingness to *confront* trouble, to withstand pain, and to battle back from formidable adversity – as does life itself at times. When things don't go your way, you have to scramble in this figurative sense. As Albert Einstein said, doing the same thing over and over again and expecting a different result is the definition of insanity. When all else fails, scrambling becomes a necessity.

In this sense scrambling is just the opposite of running away. It is facing problems head-on. It's overcoming challenges through drive and determination. It's continuing to strive for success despite discouraging setbacks. It's never giving up and never giving in – both on the field and off. Here's a great on-the-field example that some readers might remember – the Cleveland Browns' 1987 Divisional Playoff game against the New York Jets.

In the last minutes of any NFL playoff game, you are way past exhausted. You are beyond the Wall of Pain that marathoners describe at Mile 20, when the body has used up all available stored energy and begins to consume its own muscle tissue to keep going. Some of the largest, strongest, and scariest athletes in the world have been slamming into you at full force, repeatedly, for over two hours. You probably have broken some fingers or toes, at a minimum, and maybe you've had your bell rung once or twice. And if, to top it all off, you're down by two scores with less than five minutes to go, the situation might look hopeless to many people.

It certainly did to the many Browns fans who began to exit Cleveland Municipal Stadium on January 3, 1987, with the Browns down 20-10 and only 4:14 on the clock. So what do you do in this situation? You scramble. You march into the huddle on your next possession, and you tell your teammates, "We're going to take this game."

Everybody switches to scramble or survival mode. Three different receivers make five catches – Reggie Langhorne (two), Brian Brennan (two), and Curtis Dickey (one) – that get you down to the one-yard line before the two-minute warning. Your stud fullback (Kevin Mack) punches it over the goal line behind a Dan Fike block to get you to 20-17. Then your defense pushes the Jets backwards three yards in three downs to get the ball back on your own 33 with 51 seconds left. Webster Slaughter makes a nice catch off the helmet of his defender at the five-yard line. Your veteran kicker (Mark Moseley) pokes through the tying field goal with seven seconds left.

Then, in a see-saw double overtime, your defense makes three more key stops, until you can get the ball down to where your kicker can ice the game with a final field goal. Browns win, 23-20, for the team's first playoff victory in almost 20 years.

Even the *New York Times* had to concede that our comeback was "magnificent." I threw for 489 yards in that game, to 10 different teammates, with Ozzie Newsome leading the pack (114 yards on six receptions). It was a total team effort.[1] We scrambled back. Just like you often have to do in life.

I chose *"Learning to Scramble"* as the title of this book for a number of reasons. First and foremost, it describes the 'never give up' mentality of pro football. Players who don't play flat out at all times are said to be 'dogging it,' even if they are dog-tired. You're supposed to leave it all on

---

1 The 489 yards still stand as an NFL record, though I must confess that I also tossed back-to-back interceptions late in the fourth quarter to put us in that 20-10 hole. Oh well. The D's nine sacks also tied an NFL record at the time.

the field. You've heard all the clichés. They all boil down to one basic idea: professional football players must be resolute, relentless, and resilient. These attributes are what generate the intensity level that has made the game so popular. And it is this intensity which motivates my own, undying love for the game, which hopefully shines through in the pages that follow.

But *Learning to Scramble* is also a motto for life in general if you think about it, and my own life-after-football is a prime example. Anyone who has seen me in any of the ESPN *30 for 30* films (such as "The U," "The U Part 2," "Believeland," and "Broke") knows that my post-retirement career has been no bed of roses. I lost some money, but I largely gave tons of money away. Ever since I was a kid, I have operated with what I would call a brainwashed Catholicism. You know – honor thy father and thy mother and all those lessons taught in Catholic schools. As a result, I couldn't sleep at night knowing my family could use my money, so I gave boatloads of it away. I scrambled – to try to make them happy. But it didn't matter how much I gave them. In fact, the more I gave, the more they wanted – and oddly, the more they seemed to resent me. Anyway, in addition to those problems, I experienced a divorce that set a few world records for hostility. I am currently dealing with the aftermath of concussions and broken bones and ripped-up joints that would make a rodeo cowboy look soft. Life has definitely been a battle for me at times, as you shall soon see, and my limitations in the scrambling department sometimes got the better of me.

But at the end of the day, do you let them carry you off the field on a stretcher, or do you pull yourself together and fight back? I take pride in the fact that I was never carted off a football field. I always managed to get to the sidelines under my own power. That is the attitude that has gotten me through the struggles I have confronted all my life. This book, in large part, is a distillation of my own personal effort to scramble back.

I have a couple of real-life success stories to share with you concerning this 'scramble' mentality, but first I'd like to consider the origins of this mentality in relation to my life.

Where does the 'scramble' mentality come from? DNA? Maybe, to some degree; but I'm no scientist, so I can't say for sure. Upbringing? In my case, I doubt it, for reasons I'll explain later. If I had to pick a date when the concept of 'scrambling' came into my consciousness, I would go back to my college experience at the University of Miami, which is often called 'the U.'

I was a blue-collar kid from a hard-up mill town in Northeast Ohio who walked into a totally foreign environment as a third-string recruit. But before I knew it, I was quarterbacking the most unlikely group of people ever to be called a team all the way to a NCAA National Championship in the Orange Bowl. All of a sudden, thousands of people were cheering for me and my team, and millions more were rooting on TV. All of a sudden, I went from Bernie Who? to Big Man on Campus, and beyond. At the time I didn't realize how big I had become.

That '83 Hurricanes squad brought together players of every description – white, black, Hispanic, and immigrants, from every economic class – in an era and in a place when such diversity was far less common than it is now. But we forged a brotherhood that overcame all the obstacles, and in the process, we became a symbol for the whole troubled city of Miami of what could be accomplished by a group of guys who put aside their differences and scrambled back from their collective adversities.

Going from college to the pros only reinforced the necessity and importance of all that hard work. Once again, I showed up at the Cleveland Browns training camp as a raw rookie, and by the end of the season, I was leading the team I grew up worshiping to the NFL playoffs. Being a local boy, I was showered with even more adoration in Cleveland than I had experienced in Miami. I was treated like the Second Coming of Otto Graham.[2] Sell-out crowds of 80,000 were chanting my name at old Municipal Stadium, at a time when Cleveland didn't have much to cheer about. Someone wrote a song about me that blanketed the airwaves in season. I was called a civic icon. Yet, I didn't feel like an icon, nor did I believe I was anyone special. But there I was, at age 22.

It all sounds miraculous, but it wasn't easy. It took a tremendous amount of determination, preparation, resilience, and focus – all the

---

2 I personally reject any comparison to Otto Graham, whom I met several times, once on a very memorable day spent together to attend Lou Groza's funeral. Otto Graham was a quarterback for the ages. He led the Browns to the league championship in every year from 1946 through 1955, winning it in seven of those years, and he still leads the NFL in winning percentage (81.4%). For good measure, he also won a basketball championship with the Rochester Royals of the old National Basketball League (predecessor to the NBA) in 1946. When I am occasionally asked to sign a souvenir above his autograph, I always refuse. Out of respect, I only sign beneath his name. Otto Graham is in a class by himself, and I admired him greatly.

qualities I discuss in this book – to get to the mountaintop. Once there, the feeling was exhilarating, but I could never enjoy it for long. The fear of losing, for me, far outweighed the satisfaction of winning. I never felt iconic or all-powerful or anything like that. Instead, I experienced the constant pressure of giving everything I had – both mentally and physically – to be a winning NFL quarterback for my hometown team.

Outside of football, even when life sacked me hard, the scramble mentality sustained me, and still does to this day. At the end of the day, scrambling is not just a way to win football games. It is a means of facing life head-on with dedication and persistence, and tenaciously striving to overcome life's inevitable struggles or defeats.

You have all heard about the hedonistic lifestyles of professional athletes and celebrities who constantly indulge in sex, drugs, and alcohol. I'd be lying to you if I told you, at times, those were not a part of my life. But as my former coaches Howard Schnellenberger and Don Shula used to say to me, there's a time and a place for everything. They both constantly reminded me that if you do your best today, tomorrow will take care of itself.

So, before we get rolling, I have to take one thing off the table, or you may not believe anything else I tell you in this book. There is a notion that is widespread in social media and elsewhere that I must have a substance abuse problem. Usually, this is based on my speech which is slow and indistinct and, at times, borderline slurry. So when people hear me on the radio or see me on TV, they naturally wonder, "How many has he had?"

Look, in the course of 12 pro seasons in the NFL and a Division I college career at the U, not to mention high school, I had more concussions than I can remember. Officially, I had 15 in the NFL, but it was probably more like 50.

These days, after a major lawsuit by players and a billion dollar settlement, the League is taking concussions more seriously. But back in the day, no one realized the seriousness of concussions, or the ramifications in later life. They just wanted to get you back in the game.

I will have more to say about concussions later in the book. For now, here's a little mind experiment to give you a sense about the effect of concussions. Don't try this at home, but imagine running backwards 20 feet as fast as you can and slamming your head into a wall. This approximates the impact of getting slammed to the ground by a blitzing linebacker. It is only an approximation, of course, because the NFL linebackers who hit you at top speed can run 20 feet forward far faster than you can run it backward; but you get the idea. You can wear a helmet, for what that's worth. Do this several times a month for six months, every year for 20 years. Then see if your speech is any clearer than mine.

The speech problem is also a consequence of never wearing a mouth guard. Mouth guards interfered with my play-calling at the line, so I just didn't use them. As a result I broke and lost most of my teeth (especially the back ones), and from time to time, I bit off pieces of my tongue. Whatever is left of it just doesn't work as well as a tongue is supposed to. In addition, I have cracked my jaw probably a half dozen times.

There are other people who think I must be some kind of abuser because they heard I was doing the clubs on South Beach. And there was a time when I did the club thing, although as little as I could get away with. My ex-wife, Babette, loved the party scene. She liked to fox it up and hit the clubs with her celeb husband. And, like I said, I was considered a big shot in Miami, so I felt a certain sense of civic duty to get out and mingle with the fans. Personally, I preferred staying home and playing with the kids. In fact, in our first divorce records, Babette and her attorney accused me of being the "play dad" because she said all I wanted to do was stay at home with the kids and play football. I'm not really a party animal, but to appease Babette and to show a little love to the local fans, I would go out, from time to time. So yeah, there are pictures of me partying on South Beach.

Now, I won't pretend to you that I am a teetotaler. I like a cold beer as much as the next guy. And I'll have a couple drinks with people if it's in the right situation. As far as pot is concerned, you can make the case that it may be less dangerous for pro athletes than drinking. If you're at home chilling with a joint, you are far less likely to get into the kind of trouble that is all too common with jocks who go out drinking for the night and hammer down a few too many.

By the way, this is not just me talking. A small but growing number of players have recently begun urging the NFL to eliminate its ban on pot. They believe marijuana is safer as a painkiller than the approved painkilling substances. See for example the website of Eugene Moore, former offensive tackle for the Jacksonville Jaguars and Baltimore Ravens.

So I am not exactly a Puritan when it comes to booze and pot. But with that said, I have never flunked a drug test, and I have taken hundreds of them in my life. If I flunked one, I guarantee you would hear about it within hours.

The truth is that I developed a bit of a phobia about alcohol in particular, and substance abuse in general, from a very young age. My dad was very liberal with verbal abuse, even when I was a kid. For as long as I can remember, I had to listen to what a pussy I was, how kids of my day weren't as tough as kids of his day, yada-yada-yada. Just listening to it would have been bad enough, but he had to get in my face screaming, with spit flying all over. And to top it off, in mid-rant, he would send me to the kitchen to get him another beer. That's what sealed it for me. Ever since then, whenever I smell beer breath, I flash back to my dad and his tirades. Believe me, that will cure you of any temptation to drink.

I tell you all this because I know you are going to have a hard time accepting some of the things that I describe here, and you are going to wonder. All I can tell you is that I have had an incredible life. Part of why I wrote this book was to share the extremes of success and failure that I have experienced. And I'm not looking to cast stones at people, either. I like to look at life as truthfully as I possibly can – and this book is my effort to do that. I believe that facts get people closer to understanding reality, and while I've heard people say that perception is reality, I think facts get me much closer to reality than anything else. So I am going to be as truthful as I can, plain and simple.

But that's not the main reason I wrote the book. My main purpose is to share what I've learned in the process. Almost every chapter of this book, as you will see, is devoted to a virtue that I came to understand through football, or in later life. I like to think that these virtues have general relevance to everyone's experience, whatever that may be. So my ultimate hope here is that what I have gleaned from my own individual history is in some way instructive for you in pursuing your own personal victories and in confronting your own personal challenges.

Chapter 2
ATTITUDE

What does it take to be a great quarterback? The quick answer is that I don't entirely know. I do know some attributes for sure, and some of those apply to all players, not just quarterbacks, and maybe to all sports, not just football. On the other hand, there are other attributes that depend on specific characteristics and capabilities of the individual player, which are harder to explain. I even have trouble explaining my own personal idiosyncrasies, as you will see. But before we get into that, let's look at some of the general principles.

General Principle #1: I believe that success in football, at all positions – and for that matter, in all sports – requires an obsessive commitment to winning. What do I mean by obsessive? Vince Lombardi, the legendary head coach of the Green Bay Packers, said it first and said it best: "Winning isn't everything. It's the *only* thing."

Some people who aren't that familiar with the game tend to over-read that statement to mean that winning is the only thing that matters in life. I don't believe that's what Coach Lombardi meant. I am sure he valued his family and his faith and his country. Speaking as a player myself, I believe he meant something more.

In the game itself a player's sole focus has to be on winning; nothing else matters. If you are playing to get rich and live like a king, odds are you won't, at least not for very long. If your goal is to make the papers and see yourself on ESPN highlights, you're probably going to be disappointed. If you're thinking about the fans or worrying about your stats, you are doomed. The money and the fame and all the stuff that *results* from winning are actually distractions. You have to be thinking only about winning, not about what will happen to your contract, or how you will look on replay, or how you can meet hot women on the sidelines. In the game winning is the only thing you should be thinking about. If you win, the other good stuff will take care of itself. Successful players concentrate on one simple goal: win the game.

General Principle #2: You have to maintain the attitude of General Principle #1 at all times. You can't hang at a celebrity party into the wee hours the night before a game. You can't skip meetings or workouts or show up late to practice because you think you are too cool. As I mentioned before, there is a time and place for everything. It reminds me of a time during a game in the 1987 season which we were losing at halftime. I prayed (or maybe made a deal?) to God that if we came back to win, I wouldn't have sex the rest of the season. Remember, I live with what I call "brainwashed Catholicism." I'm not saying what I did was right, but it shows how focused I was on winning. For the record, we did come back and win the game, and within an hour after the game, I was looking for a loophole in my prayers to the Big Guy. Not everybody goes to those extremes, to be sure, but you get the idea. You judge all your behavior by whether it will help or hurt your ability to win ball games.

I prayed constantly for football success, and I'm not sure that was really right in the spirit of prayer. But being the brainwashed Catholic boy, prayer was a key part of my life, and winning was so important to me. For me, I was never more religious than when I was between the white lines playing football.

These two general principles depend, in part, on your ability to block out distractions and stay focused on your primary objective. That same idea applies specifically to success at the quarterback position. For example, in a pass play, you have to be able to block out of your mind any concern about what will happen to you after you release the ball. You cannot think about the bone-jarring hits you will receive from the pass rushers. You can tell when a quarterback is thinking about that by looking at his feet. If his feet are in constant motion, what we call 'nervous feet,' he's worried about getting hit and not totally focused on completing his pass.

You can say the same thing about nervous eyes. In my opinion the proper sequence is to look downfield first. If everybody is covered, then you look short. If your eyes are shooting all over the place, that is called bewilderment, or more likely, raw fear.

I'm not saying you ignore the defense – that would be suicidal. But there are times when you just have to stand in there, knowing you are going to get hammered, and make the play without thinking about the contact, especially if you are slow. There were many times when I knew I was going to get blasted, but I also knew that the pass rusher was going to be just a split second too late to stop me from releasing. I actually took pleasure – joy, even – in making those completions because I knew in that nano-second between the release and the hit that I had beaten my opponent. Those little mini-thrills were a huge part of my love for the game. I can't describe the satisfaction I got from beating the best, especially when it was just by a hair. It was euphoric.

One of my favorite examples of this occurred while I was playing for the NFC Championship with Dallas in 1993. When the Browns cut me after week eight, Jimmy Johnson, head coach of the Cowboys, immediately picked me up to back up Troy Aikman. Late in the third quarter of the NFC title game against San Francisco, Aikman got hit so hard he couldn't remember his plays anymore (according to Johnson) and had to leave the game. The Niners were breathing fire. After a bad start they had come back to within two scores, and after knocking Aikman out of the game, they were determined to put me in the hospital and continue their comeback.

Keep in mind that at this point, I had been with the Cowboys for a grand total of 10 weeks. I was still learning their playbook and their team vernacular (every team has different codes for play-calling) and getting to know the guys. Then I get called out of the bullpen to save a championship for them. We were on our own 19, with the rest of the team bummed out about losing their star quarterback.

On a key third-down play, San Francisco came with everything. I got off a 12-yard completion for a first down to Michael Irvin (who I actually knew from the U). A couple plays later, I assumed that the 49ers would be in all-out blitz mode on third and 10. But I also figured that the secondary would be seriously depleted because everybody would be coming after me.

As soon as the ball was snapped, they came in force. I spotted Cowboys receiver Alvin Harper, and flipped it to him. Thanks to the depleted secondary, Alvin romped untouched for a 42-yard touchdown, which pretty much iced the game and sent the Cowboys to Super Bowl XXVIII.[3]

---

3 I didn't get to start the Super Bowl. Aikman healed up and came back for that game. But I did get to play, technically. Jimmy Johnson sent me in to take a knee on the last play so that I could tell my grandchildren that I had played in a Super Bowl. I always thought that was a classy move on Jimmy's part. Plus, I got a Super Bowl ring for my contribution to the overall effort. I also managed to commandeer that last game ball after I took the knee.

You can still see this completion on YouTube. What you won't see is what happened to me after the throw. I wound up buried under 600 pounds of defensive beef. I didn't immediately notice that I had two teeth knocked out until I realized that I was chewing one of them. I must have swallowed the other one.

My two assailants taunted me without mercy. "We yoked you! We yoked you! Y'all can't play!" But even before I could get up and see what had happened, I could hear 80,000 Cowboy fans cheering wildly. So I calmly replied, "Yeah, you got me good. But I don't think all those Dallas fans are cheering for you." Those are the moments that made it all worthwhile.

You pay a price, of course, in the form of busted teeth and worse. But you can't think about that while you're making the play. I realize this is not normal human behavior. Normal human behavior calls for being *very* worried when a freight train is charging toward you. So what's the secret? I can't really break it down into a 'how-to' recipe for blocking out fear. I can only suggest that maybe in my case I had a special 'gift' for this because of my upbringing. I spent my whole childhood taking constant abuse from my dad. Later on, I was subjected to all kinds of unpleasant demands from my family and friends (I'll go into the details later). So when you grow up constantly bombarded in this way, you learn to block things out. You know there are going to be painful consequences, but you learn not to think about them because otherwise, you would go crazy. If you think that sounds pitiful, consider this: I had a lot of success in the NFL because of my ability to screen out the anticipation of pain. If you don't learn to block out the pain, you won't win.

The subject of pain brings us to **General Principle #3:** For all practical purposes, pain does not exist in football – not for quarterbacks, not for anybody. This may sound absurd, at first, because we've all seen players writhing in pain on the field after a severe injury. Yes, an incapacitating injury is an exception, but short of an immobilizing injury, pain cannot stop you.

I myself once played three quarters of a game on a broken ankle. I wouldn't even acknowledge the pain. To acknowledge pain is to allow self-doubt to creep into your consciousness, so you just don't do it. I did have to acknowledge that I couldn't put any weight on my ankle, but what the hell: as I said before, I was never a scrambler anyway. Besides, I didn't need my ankle to throw, so why wouldn't I keep playing?

Marty Schottenheimer used to yell at me, "Don't lie to me! Tell me when you're hurt!" What Coach Schottenheimer didn't understand was that I wasn't lying to him. I was lying to myself. I simply denied to myself that I was ever too hurt to play. If you asked me if I were ready to go, the answer was, "Hell yeah!" That's just how it is in our game. It's not so much a macho thing or a high pain-threshold thing as it is a mind-over-matter thing. You're so laser-focused on winning the game that you just don't pay attention to the pain.

Now, before I leave you with the impression that all NFL players are Zen masters at feats of mind-over-matter, let me quickly point out that we had a lot of help from the chemical sciences, specifically pharmacology. Cortisone and Toradol injections were commonplace, to reduce joint and muscle inflammation. Toradol is now a banned substance in the NFL. But in my day, a pre-game shot was routine; I'd guess maybe 30% of players would also get a booster shot at halftime.

You never really knew what you were getting with those injections. Everything was called 'cortisone,' but the post-game shots we would get on Sundays and Mondays had a little extra somethin-somethin laced in. In fact, the favorite additions were Darvon, Vicodin, and Oxycodone. I didn't know at the time that these were narcotics. I just knew that they let me continue to play.

If the narcotics and the anti-inflammatories didn't work for players, there were always other options available. Painkillers were in constant supply in the trainer's room or the locker room. Consumption was 'self-regulated.' In other words, help yourself.

Even back in my day, there was a League drug policy of sorts. But the list of banned substances was nowhere near as long or as specific as it is today. Furthermore, there was no random testing. We peed in the cup only once a year, at the end of training camp, and everybody knew it. So all you had to do was remember in early July to stop using whatever it was you were into in order to give your body a month or so to cleanse. Then you were good to go for the next 10 months, which of course included the regular season and the playoffs.

I hadn't known a thing about painkillers and injections. After breaking a couple of fingers during a college game, I had been given a shot in my left hand. I hadn't wanted the shot, but the team doctor and coach insisted it would be best for me. Unfortunately, the doctor accidentally hit a nerve, which numbed my entire left side, including my left arm.

So you can see why I was hesitant to take injections. But this changed in my first pro season after I got cracked hard by Lawrence Taylor and Carl Banks and broke some ribs. So I took a shot to finish the game. From then on it became more and more routine. When the lion's share of 53 guys are lined up every game to get their shots, it almost seemed like I didn't put the team first if I didn't get a dose. And I never wanted to be labeled one of those guys.

Normally, drug administration took place in the locker room – that is to say, out of sight of the general public. But not always. I once got a shot on the sideline, during a game, after I had broken my ankle. They laid me out on a bench and threw a blanket over me while a bunch of our biggest guys stood around me to block the view. The networks didn't have as many cameras rolling back then as they do now, so the TV audience didn't get to see this.

My worst shot was an injection with a huge-ass horse needle through the bottom of my foot, given to me to treat a plantar fascia injury. Oh Lord, that hurt. I think I might have preferred the hit from LT and Banks. Shots through the kneecap were no fun either. I got one once to reduce inflammation around a partially torn ACL (anterior cruciate ligament). In those days before arthroscopic surgery, these shots were the only answer for all kinds of knee problems ranging from a frayed ligament to a torn meniscus. The needle was also the weapon of choice for draining fluids from swollen ankles and knees.

In addition to all the other medications, I used to keep smelling salts on me at all times during games. Smelling salts are basically a nose hit of ammonia, and they are a banned substance now. But back in the day, when I got my bell rung, they came in really handy to snap me out of a daze. Today, those incidents would probably be diagnosed as concussions, and I would be immediately taken out of the game and put into a concussion protocol.

While I did accept the necessity of certain medications, I drew the line at steroids, but not for any moral or legal reasons. I was afraid steroids might mess up my throwing. At the same time I would have been perfectly willing to pay for steroids for my linemen (I never actually did). I wanted them to pack on as much muscle mass as possible. Again, I'm not saying it was right, but my will to win was enormous. It reminds me of the many coaches I had who would say to my teammates and me that if you're not cheating, you're not trying to win and you don't want to win badly enough.

As I grew older, the aches and pains got worse and more frequent, so I progressively took more and more shots as I neared the end of my career. Lord only knows what long term damage they did to my body. I'm still taking treatments to flush all the poison out of my body. But poisons let me play, and that was my burning ambition.

To play quarterback, you obviously need certain physical skills in addition to the attitudes I have been discussing. You have to be able to throw the rock where you're aiming it. But the important part here is the accuracy and timing of your throws. Lots of guys can heave the ball an incredible distance. The key, though, is hitting a receiver who is moving extremely fast through a thicket of defenders who are also moving extremely fast, in such a way that the defenders can't catch the ball first. And, you have to do it over and over again. It appears that this was my gift. I might be able to give you some pointers on reading defenses, but I can't teach you hand-eye coordination. You either have it or you don't. Also, I probably would not be the best coach of form and technique. I threw every which way but loose. It worked for me, but nobody ever considered my form to be 'classic.'

One other physical gift that helped me, I'm sure, was exceptional peripheral vision. Jerry Glanville, the former head coach of the Houston Oilers, used to say that wherever Bernie's eyes were looking, he'd throw somewhere else. That gift helped, given my limited speed, and it gave my receivers that extra step or two on their defenders. Anyway, that kind of vision comes in handy when you're trying to find receivers, or just as important, trying to dodge pass rushers coming up on your blind side.

But in the end, physical gifts (other than throwing accuracy) are less important than you may think. As most football fans may recall, I was never a particularly gifted athlete. In college I struggled to bench press 225 pounds. Vinny Testaverde, who was my teammate at Miami and who quarterbacked the Hurricanes and the Browns after me, could bench twice that much. I ran the 40-yard dash in 5.45 seconds. NFL defensive backs can run the 40 *backwards* faster than that. I was fairly tall, at 6'5," but skinny by NFL standards. I worked out like a madman to develop cardio strength and stamina; but muscle strength and speed were just not in my DNA.

What I could do was read the X's and O's, or rather, as you will see in the next chapter, the M's and the S's and the W's and all the other symbols that represent defensive players in the graphic schemes used to diagram and analyze football plays. Nobody could internalize those diagrams better than I could. And I don't just mean during the *chalk talks*, the team meetings where coaches would diagram plays and situations on a chalk board. I mean on the field. I was like Neo in *The Matrix*. Players on the field were just so many symbols in the playbook to me, streaming through my consciousness, like Neo reading blizzards of green machine code to make out the 'reality' of the Matrix at hyper-speed. This mental aspect of football is key, particularly for a quarterback.

Again, I can't provide a step-by-step program for how you learn this. For me, it just came naturally. I was always good in math at school, I have never needed a calculator, and I gravitated to math-type courses in college, like finance and economics. I'm sure that my love of numbers had something to do with my success in the NFL. So for all you slow, skinny, wall-eyed, obsessive math nerds out there with good aim who are indifferent to pain and who aspire to be quarterbacks, I am living proof that there may be hope for you.

Chapter 3
INTELLIGENCE

For a long time baseball has traditionally been considered to be the thinking man's game, and football, to be an exercise in brutality. The columnist George Will, whom I have met personally on a number of occasions, and whose work I often enjoy, is a devoted baseball fan and a true believer in this tradition. He has gone so far as to claim that football represents the two worst aspects of American culture: extreme violence, punctuated by committee meetings (i.e., huddles).

With all due respect to Mr. Will, I take exception to this traditional view. These notions may have been valid back in the 1950's, when baseball was experiencing its Golden Age, and football was just emerging from the leather helmet era as a major sport. But that was 60-some years ago. Personally, I believe those ideas are way outdated.

Don't get me wrong. I played baseball when I was a kid, all the way through high school, and I was pretty good. So I am not a baseball basher. In fact, I love the game. But football has come a long way in 60 years.

Consider, for instance, Coach Bill Belichick of the New England Patriots and former coach of the Browns. Everybody knows I was never happy to be unceremoniously cut from the Browns by Belichick in mid-season (more on this later). But the reality is that he and I have moved past that and talk to each other regularly. In fact, I am flattered that he thinks enough of my opinions to call me every so often. The man really is a football genius and a prime example of my theory that football truly has become the thinking man's sport. Did you know that Belichick graduated from an Ivy League-type college (Wesleyan, in Connecticut)?

Some of my argument is based on obvious facts about the game. Think about the intellectual effort that goes into a single football game. Every sport, of course, analyzes film and statistics. But no other sport has a whole week to analyze and prepare for every game. Baseball plays 162 games in a six-month season. That's five and a half games a week, on average, to football's one. Baseball players are lucky if they get one off-day per month when they aren't travelling. Do you think they're studying film on their one off-day or hitting the links?

Or consider team size. A football roster has twice as many players as a baseball roster, and three times as many positions (33, counting offense, defense, and special teams, versus nine, or 10 with the DH). How many more permutations and combinations does that make when designing plays? On top of that, with virtually all plays in football, certain players have multiple options to choose from in mid-play, depending on how the opponent sets up and executes. See, for example, the extended discussion of *92 Lex Flanker Zid* in the next chapter.

Next, consider the size of the coaching staffs. Larger rosters and more positions in football mean more coaches and assistants studying, plotting, and instructing. The New England Patriots, for all their success, actually have the least number of paid assistant coaches in the League. They have around 15 coaches. Most teams have more than 20, making the League average probably around 2.5 players for every coach (How is that for a student-to-teacher ratio?). Considering these numbers alone, more thought goes into a football game than a baseball game, by a significant multiple.

Add to that the nature of the schedule and the challenge of scouting. With 162 games and an unbalanced schedule, a baseball manager will know some of his divisional rivals almost as well as his own team. Not a lot of surprises to contemplate, nor a lot of time to do the contemplating. In the NFL, by contrast, division rivals are the only teams you see more than once – twice, to be exact, at different times in the season. So virtually every game is a new challenge. The army of coaches mentioned above will spend all week studying film of the opposition's strengths and vulnerabilities, drawing up a game plan, and developing elaborate play lists. There are substitutions on virtually every play. The thought process is like a chess match. The only difference for football players, of course, is the threat of death or dismemberment.

When I first showed up at Browns training camp, they handed me a playbook that was thicker than this book. It was 242 pages long, mostly diagrams of formations and play options, with some pages having a dozen different diagrams. I actually counted them all up: over 1,500 diagrams, and that didn't exhaust all the options – it just showed examples. And the diagrams aren't just written with X's and O's – that's Pop Warner stuff. On these diagrams every position and every "concept" has a code. Linebackers, for example, are M (Mike) for middle linebacker, S (Sam) for strong side outside linebacker, W (Will) for weak side linebacker, and sometimes B (Buck), who would be the weak side middle linebacker in a 3-4 defense (3 linemen, 4 backers), with Will shifting to the outside.

To give you a sense of magnitude, there were 18 chapters in the Browns *offensive* playbook (why couldn't it be 19?), covering all aspects of that half of the game. There were five chapters devoted just to line blocking.[4] There was a whole chapter devoted to screen passes that diagrammed 117 different possibilities, with names like *Rip-Liz 589 Slow* and *Lee-Ray 564 Read*. It was a lot for a rookie to digest in a few weeks.

As a player I always did my best to do my part. In season I was 1,000% football. I would dream about football in my sleep. I kept a pencil and notepad on my nightstand for when I would wake up thinking I should call *Rip Liz 589 Slow* on second and long because the Bears blitz 76% of the time in that situation.

If I wasn't at practice or in the workout room or the trainer's room, I was watching film: watching at the Stadium, watching at my house, watching whenever and wherever I could. In fact by the time I got to the Stadium on Monday morning, I had watched the previous day's game at least three times already, and at least two games of our upcoming opponent. It's a good thing they didn't have video screens in cars back then, or I would have been watching while driving.

As a side note, I know that my singular focus on football caused problems. To be fair, as soon as I started seeing success and happiness in football, I was aggressively up front with people about the primary importance of football in my life. It was my #1 priority. When I finally had a chance to leave home (to go to the U) and compete in the sport I loved so much, and when I first entered the League in Cleveland, I had the opportunity to simply play football and I performed pretty well. When I finally gave in to family and friends' complaints about my obsessive focus, my career and personal life suffered a bit. Maybe I was wrong to focus on

---

4 As much fun as it was to throw the ball, it all starts with the core. Both offensive and defensive lines have to be on the same page and physically dominant for consistent, long-term success.

football so much, but for a poor kid from a poor family in Youngstown who had an opportunity to play in the NFL, I felt I needed to give everything I had to it. I didn't want to wake up one day at age 55 and wonder, "what if?"

The purpose of all this film study was to calculate the opponent's tendencies. On first and 10, for example, the Steelers blitz X% of the time when the offense is backed up inside the 20, Y% when the offense is at midfield, Z% when the offense is in the red (or, as many people like Coach Shula used to call it, "green" – because that's where you made all your money) zone. But that's just one, oversimplified example. My ultimate objective was to develop a spreadsheet, if you will, of tendencies on how the defense would set up in all kinds of situations, based on a number of factors.

The first factor was the down and yardage situation. What do they like to do on first and 10? First and 15? Second and long? Second and three to seven? Second and minus three? Third and long? Third and three to seven? Etc., etc., etc. Figure on over 20 or so down/yardage possibilities in all.

Then, you had to recalibrate all these possibilities based on field position. Are you in your own territory? Backed up? Or in their territory? Deep? Or mid-field somewhere? Call it 10 sets of possibilities for field position.

You also have to take personnel into consideration. Different players have different capabilities and tendencies. Where does the defense have rookies or back-ups? Where do they have Pro Bowlers? What are the tendencies of individual players in all these various situations?

Then, you have clock considerations. What do they do early in the game? What adjustments do they make at halftime? Late in the game?

Finally, the score matters. A defense that is defending a two-point lead with two minutes to go will be different from a defense that is up by three touchdowns. Or down by two points. Or by two touchdowns.

Get the picture? There are a lot of situations to figure out: at a minimum, many hundreds. And by 'figure out,' I mean three things. First of all, you have to figure out all your opponent's tendencies in those several hundred situations. This is why I spent most of my Mondays and all of my Tuesdays (theoretically, our 'off-day'), as well as all my other spare time, studying film. Coaches would typically review film from the opponent's last three games in order to glean these tendencies. I would watch the last four, just to be sure I wasn't missing something. And the playoffs give you the opportunity to watch the whole season.

Then, after you figured out the opponent, you have to figure out what you're going to do about it. What plays are you going to call in all these situations? Remember, you have hundreds of options to choose from.

Third, you have to burn all this information into your brain deeply enough so that you can remember it all in the heat of battle, after you have been pummeled half to death and have had your bell rung a few times, or as happened to me once, after you have had your ankle broken in the first quarter of a Monday night game.

In retrospect figuring out all this stuff wasn't so different from the kind of analysis that Bill James introduced in baseball, and that Billy Beane and Paul DePodesta[5] used with such success for the Oakland A's in the early 2000's, as memorialized in the book and the movie *Money Ball.* Nowadays, that sort of analysis is becoming more talked about in football. In my day we didn't have much in the way of computers (and no Internet), so it was considerably more difficult.

I personally got into the analysis big time, partly because I would do anything to win, but also because I was a dyed-in-the-wool numbers nut. I would take copious notes while watching film, then do the math (in my head) to calculate opposition tendencies into percentages, then fill out my mental spreadsheet of possibilities, and ultimately start contemplating countermeasures. I actually had fun doing this. So call me a nerd.

In my playing days the media liked to refer to my football 'intelligence.' I'm not sure they knew what they meant by that. I think it had more to do with my lack of any obvious athletic skills that would explain my high completion rate, or our offense's general success. I couldn't run worth a damn, I threw from every conceivable angle, and I often looked pretty clumsy in the process. So it must have been something intellectual, right?

I have never thought of myself as an intellectual. Maybe I should take credit for this, since God knows I've been blamed for enough things that weren't my fault. But seriously, I just can't picture myself as the professor type. Furthermore, if you met me in person, I guarantee you would say, "This guy graduated from college? In two and a half years? No way."

I will take credit, however, at least partially, for one particular football innovation: the fake spike. Gary Danielson and I came up with this little

---

5 In 2016 the Browns hired DePodesta as Chief Strategy Officer, in a bold effort to translate *Money Ball* magic into the football world. Interestingly, DePodesta's first job was as a scout for the Cleveland Indians.

beauty toward the beginning of my career when Gary and I became close friends. He was like my player-coach. He and I, who both believe strongly in never wasting a play, were watching film together of a late-game spike (to stop the clock), and an idea popped into my head. What if, instead of actually spiking the ball, the quarterback *pretended* to spike the ball but then dropped back and flicked a pass? Since the defense usually just stands around when the QB spikes the ball, a receiver should be wide open somewhere. If you see a rookie cornerback on the defense, that's even better. Rookies are the most likely to be babe-watching the stands in that situation, instead of attending to business, so you throw there.

Gary liked my idea, so we started practicing the play with the Browns. I even pulled it out once, in that crazy, double-overtime playoff game against the New York Jets in the 1986 post-season. When we had the ball on the one with less than a minute left in regulation, it seemed like the perfect situation for the fake spike. We tried it, but unfortunately, the pass was incomplete, so that attempt never made the history books.

Fast forward eight years, by which point I was near the end of my career, backing up Dan Marino with the Miami Dolphins. With Coach Shula's blessing, I was calling a lot of the offensive plays in those days, and after all those years of waiting for just the right situation for the fake spike, we finally got our chance. In a key game against the Jets, the Dolphins were down 24-21, with 38 seconds left, and the ball on the Jets 8-yard line. A chip shot field goal would have tied the game and sent it into overtime, and that's what everybody in the stadium expected.

So I signaled for the fake spike. Marino hustled up to the line and yelled "Clock, clock, clock" to help sell the charade. Then he took the snap, faked the spike, and while the defense lolled around, he tossed a pillow to his receiver, hitting Mark Ingram for an easy touchdown and the victory. This game has become known as The Clock Game, and every team in the NFL now practices the fake spike.

And if mind games qualify as intellectual, some called me Einstein. I tried to mess with people's heads and felt like I had to in order to be successful. Early in games I sometimes taunted defenders with trash like, "You suck so bad, I'm throwing the rock right at your sorry ass!" Of course they didn't believe me. I had to be trying to trick them, right? So the last thing they expected was for me to throw the rock right at their sorry asses, which is exactly what I did. Then, after I'd burned them five or six times with this little gambit, I did it again late in the game. The defense doesn't want to look stupid a seventh time, so this time they believed me. Only this time, I called something different in the huddle and beat them again. I loved making defenses crazy like that. It maximized the chance of being successful on each play.

One time, I took particular pleasure in pulling this ruse on Greg Lloyd, a linebacker for the Pittsburgh Steelers, in his rookie year. He was a phenomenal talent at linebacker, but he did too much chirping and name-calling for a rookie. You need to show a little respect for your elders. So I did my "You suck" routine on him, and we won that game. For a kid from Youngstown, it felt amazing to beat the Steelers.

In those days the Steelers had Rod Woodson at cornerback, who was all-time all-everything at his position. I also played against incredible players like Ronnie Lott, Deion Sanders, and others. While they were great players, I believed you had to throw at them. You had to have faith in what you and your teammates could do. While you had to mix up routes and always be hyper aware of these great defenders, you still needed to throw their way to maintain credibility with the team and open up the field. Don't get me wrong – I knew how difficult this was, but usually I coached up our receivers the entire week before a game, reminding them they could do it once kickoff rolled around. But I did relish the opportunities to tell less stellar counterparts at cornerback, "I don't even know your name." That got under their skin like poison ivy.

Pre-season was a great time for head games. You run plays or do stuff in pre-season that you would never do in regular season. But you plant a seed, an expectation in the mind of everyone who watches film of that game, of what your propensities are in that certain situation – you know, mixing in different personnel groups and various plays that probably won't be a part of the game plan when the real season starts.

I also loved stealing signs from the defense, and I got pretty good at it. Typically, I had about 15 seconds to kill after each play before we huddled, while our coaches strategized with each other about what to call next. I used this time to look for the defensive signal caller on the sidelines to see what the opposition was thinking. Then I'd watch for patterns: fist pumps, hand to head, to hip, to thigh, whatever, not unlike baseball signs from a third base coach. I couldn't decode everything, of course. But I could figure out, for example, that a whole lot of motion probably meant some kind of man coverage/blitz. So I was pretty good at 'football counter-intelligence.'

Then there was 'counter-counter' intelligence. I had a range of vocal and hand signals that I used at the line to change a play when I saw something in the defensive set-up. Typically, a closed fist with a look to a receiver meant a bomb; a slashing motion meant a slant; pointing a finger like a gun meant a stutter move; a hand behind the back, after one of these other signals, meant a 'lock,' which meant "Do it no matter what." There were many others, but you get the basic idea.

Over time, however, and sometimes in the course of a single game, defensive coordinators (and some players) would get the hang of my signals and start to counter-intelligence *me*. So I would have to change it up. I would do fake calls. I would tell Webster Slaughter, for example, "If I yell at you and show the slash (which normally meant slant), it means bomb. So if I yell at you, no matter what I yell, and I show you the slash, go deep, OK?" That's counter-counter intelligence.

With all the play variations, the prior planning, the mind games, the counter-intelligence, and the counter-counter intelligence, football can get ridiculously complex. For that very reason I often had to go in the opposite direction and take steps to simplify things. When you have so many things on your mind, and you're hurt and you're tired, it's easy to lose track of the obvious. So I had a rule that when the defense presents you with a gift, you simply take the gift.

For example, if you have a 5'10" defender matching up against your 6'5" receiver, you don't need a Nobel Prize to figure out where to throw the ball. It's not that hard. Throw it to the big guy. Feed the Big Dawg. Let the Big Dawg eat, as I liked to say.

If you get up to the line and see seven defenders bunched up on the side where you were planning to run, you check off and run in the other direction. It's not that hard. Your coaches may get mad, but your running backs really appreciate it when you don't feed them to the lions.

For similar reasons I developed a play I refer to as The Look play. I called this play without an audible signal; I just gave certain receivers a particular half-crazed look when we were in the set. When I gave them The Look, they knew exactly what to do. No permutations and combinations, just one simple route we had rehearsed a million times. When it's late in the fourth quarter, and receivers are exhausted and banged up, and 80,000 fans are screaming so loud it makes their heads throb, they thank the Lord (and their QB) for a break from all the thinking.

That said, I was told all my career that the coaches were on the sidelines guessing what the other coaches were calling. Schnellenberger always reminded me that I was the last player to see the defense and that I should trust my own judgment. Of course, coaches put a lot of effort into their play lists. The truth is, I had usually worked up my own playlists (see p. 76-78) and practiced it with the team on Thursdays and Fridays after we had finished rehearsing whatever the coaches wanted. Let me just share with you here a couple of contrasting examples of coaching styles.

As I have mentioned, my coach at the University of Miami was Schnellenberger, who coached under Bear Bryant at Alabama and Don Shula at Baltimore and Miami. Shula, in turn, had played for Paul Brown in the glory days of the Cleveland Browns. All these guys were old school. They believed that the quarterback was supposed to overcome all obstacles to victory, including, if necessary, bad coaching.

In a national title game against Nebraska, we were up by a touchdown but backed up on our own one-yard line. In that situation, everybody runs, to give themselves a little breathing room. Nobody likes to throw from the end zone because it's too dangerous. And in fact, in the huddle, I called a run.

But when I got to the line, I saw that most of the defense was jammed up front to stop the run, and that the cornerback covering Downtown Eddie Brown,[6] our phenom receiver, was off him more than 10 yards and had what we call a hard inside technique. So I checked off and called for an out pattern.

Now, most quarterbacks don't call for an out pattern in that situation. That's just asking for a pick six (an interception that is easily run back for a touchdown), which would have tied the game in this case. But that's what I called. I threw it maybe seven yards to Eddie, he ran it for another six or so, and boom – we had breathing room. When I got back to the bench, I got a high five from Coach Schnellenberger.[7] And back then, nobody got high fives from him.

Fast forward 10 years to my last game with the Browns. It was late in a game against Denver, and I had been watching the Bronco safeties creep up

---

6 Eddie went on to have a terrific 10-year career with the Cincinnati Bengals. Nobody could cover him at the college level, and he was a huge factor in my own success at the U.
7 I had actually gone to the bench before the play for some help from Coach Schnellenberger. His advice: "Do whatever the fuck is right!" I loved that guy.

little by little all afternoon. So while we were still on the sidelines, I pulled over my receiver Michael Jackson and drew up a play in the dirt. I wanted him to go 18 yards, do a two-step square-in to draw the safeties, and then break deep. It worked like a charm. The safeties closed on the square-in and then watched helplessly while Jackson broke deep. Touchdown. The next day, Bill Belichick cut me from the Browns. He cited my 'diminished skills,' but I'm sure my sandlot free-lancing might have had something to do with it.

In fairness to Coach Belichick, he was new, and therefore, perhaps a little touchy about his command and control. I can assure you that is no longer the case. A significant part of the success the New England Patriots have enjoyed, since Belichick has been there, comes from his complete confidence in his quarterback to do the right thing, even if on the fly. Of course, such confidence may come easier if your quarterback is young Tom Brady, and not old Bernie Kosar.

Anyway, the point of my contrasting tales is to illustrate the concept of football intelligence. I once heard General Wesley Clark say that there are two kinds of battle plans: the kind that might work, and the kind that won't work. There's no such thing as a plan that will work because you can't read the enemy's mind, and you can't anticipate everything. You have to be able to adapt. I think this same idea applies to game plans.

So even though I was a huge devotee of studying film and creating statistical spreadsheets of defensive tendencies; even though I engaged in constant mental gymnastics over offensive alternatives; and even though I loved playing on-field head games and sign recognition; I also realized there were times when you had to chuck all the stats and the out-thinking and the master plan and invoke the KISS principle: Keep It Simple, Stupid. Even when all hell was breaking loose, and the sideline brain trust was screaming and scrambling to salvage their game plan, I was still able to recognize the obvious.

This principle is particularly true late in the game. It is my seasoned observation that late in games, when players are beyond drained, and coaches are seizing up with brain cramps, people tend to revert to their most basic tendencies. Going down to the wire in a tight game, Buddy Ryan of the Chicago Bears was not going to lose with a zone defense. You could count on the blitz. The chess game was over. So I would just call our standard offense against the 46 defense. That's keeping it simple – at least mentally. You still have to pull it off in the play, which can be a tall order.

And in the end maybe that's the secret to intelligence, of the football variety or otherwise. Yes, you have to do your homework. You have to master all the permutations and combinations, and consider all the possibilities. But in the end you also have to be able to distill all your homework and brain strain down to something manageable and useful that you can actually apply, or adapt, in real-life situations. You may be able to recite the whole Bible, from Genesis 1:1 through the end of Revelation. But that in itself does not make you religious, or shall we say, 'religion intelligent.' It really doesn't mean anything unless you can also boil it all down to some basic principles to live by and put into action, even in the teeth of adversity. And you can count on adversity in your life, even if you don't play football.

It all comes down to this: intelligence isn't about making simple things seem complicated. It's about making complicated things seem simple.

Chapter 4
PREPARATION

In case the last chapter didn't persuade you that football is the thinking man's game, I am going to break down one of my favorite plays for you: the *92 Lex Flanker Zid Halfback Chip Check Through* against the *Weak Eagle Cover 4*. Can I see a show of hands of people who understand what I just said?

Let me translate, going backwards. The *Weak Eagle Cover 4* is a plain vanilla defense. Though I usually prayed for a blitz defense so I could hit for the big score, even base defenses like the *Weak Eagle Cover 4* provided opportunities for a considerable gain. If I did not see a blitz, I hoped that I would see this defense in undisguised form, which I probably did five or ten percent of the time (i.e., six or eight plays per game). *Cover 4* means that all the defensive backs drop back into pass coverage, with each one covering one quarter of the field. *Weak Eagle* refers to the fact that the weak side linebacker (aka Will) is probably going to blitz or rush the quarterback.[8] This basic alignment is shown below:

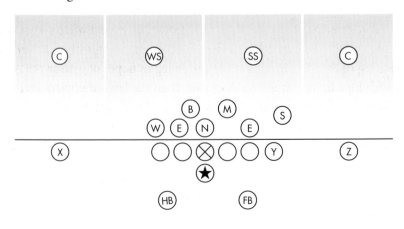

Flanker Zid was our code for a deep post pattern by the flanking receiver to the tight end (Y) side. A deep post calls for the flanker to fly down the sideline and break for the goal post, with some subtleties that I will get into shortly. The flanker on the right side is known as the Z receiver, and he's going deep, hence Z-i-D (Z Deep). You can't come up to the line and yell "Hey Z, run the post!" No defense is that dumb.

Lex informs the inside receiver, in this case the tight end (Y), what his route is, which we will get into in a moment.

The *92* clues in the linemen. The *90* tells them their blocking assignments – and for this play, it meant they will slide to the left. The 2 tells them that the tight end is lined up on the right. Every play in football is encoded in this way, partly because you don't have time to recite three paragraphs of instructions to 10 other guys, and partly to keep the other teams from knowing your intentions. Accordingly, each team has a different code.

I loved *92 Lex Flanker Zid* because it contains a lot of options. The primary receiver is Z because what you're hoping for is a long gain or even a touchdown. For this reason Z is considered the '1' concept in this play.

In the Cover 4 the cornerbacks (CB's) line up just across the line from the X and Z receivers. Cornerbacks are trained to employ outside technique, meaning that their job is to defend the deep quarter of the field from the outside. The inside break (i.e., the post route) is presumed to be covered by the strong safety (SS) and CB. So at the snap, Z runs the post, pushing the CB outside and forcing the CB to turn his hips outside at the post breaking point (which is typically 12 – 18 yards from the line of scrimmage), aiming at the inside post of the goal post. If the play feature I'm about to describe succeeds in pulling the SS out of position, Z should be open deep, or at least in a one-on-one situation.

In order to freeze the SS in position and keep him out of deep coverage against Z, Y (the tight end) runs upfield 12-14 yards, eventually at the inside leg of the SS. He runs at the inside leg in hopes of getting the SS to turn his hips inside. If the SS does this, then the laws of physics makes it much harder for him to turn back to the outside and get deep.

But to accomplish this, Y must first get around Sam, the outside linebacker across the line from him. In order to get past Sam, Y takes a

---

8 For the uninitiated, the 'strong side' is the side where the tight end (Y) lines up because he becomes the third lineman (although he might have receiving assignments, as in *92 Lex Flanker Zid*) on that side of the center.

step outside at the snap, to get Sam to turn outside, then cuts inside and runs at the SS.

Y's objective, however, is not to block the SS. Rather, he has two alternative goals. One, as noted, is to draw the SS into covering him and not Z. The other is to run an intermediate passing route. He is therefore the '2' receiver in this situation. At the 12-14 yard distance, he will cut 90° to the inside. If I am getting rushed hard, I might throw to him there when he makes his cut. If not, Y will cut across the middle and across the face of the SS (this is a cardinal rule of inside breaking routes in my system). He should still be available for a throw, depending on how the defense reacts.

Following directly behind Y is the fullback (FB), who is the '3' concept in this play. The FB will follow Y, practically on his butt, about six yards past the line and then circle in toward the middle. In the lingo this is known as a 'fullback circle' or 'fullback option.' The play development, prior to Y and the FB making their breaks, is shown below:

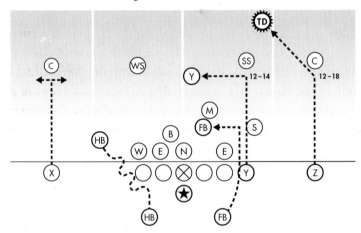

Now, with Y and the FB coming through the right side, the defense on that side has some decisions to make. They don't know which directions Y and the FB are going to go. Normally, Mike (the middle linebacker) would cover anyone who broke inside, and Sam would cover whoever broke outside. But what do they do when both the 2 and 3 receivers break in the same direction? In this case with both breaking to the inside, Sam will be trying to catch up from behind, which takes him out of the picture. Mike cannot cover both the 2 and the 3, so one of them will be open unless the SS gets involved. But if the SS gets involved, he, like Sam, will be trailing the play, and Z will then be open for his post.

Meanwhile, on the other side of the field, additional options are developing. The X receiver (left flanker) runs downfield 18 yards, exactly, and then runs a comeback (to the outside) or a hook (to the inside). Personally, I always preferred the comeback, where there is less traffic. Downfield, inside moves tend to expose receivers to more tacklers moving at much higher speeds. Getting receivers killed makes the quarterback very unpopular with the surviving receivers and is generally bad for business, so I tended to avoid hanging my receivers out to dry over the middle.

Last but not least, in case all else fails, I have a halfback (HB) to use as an outlet receiver. The HB's job is twofold. His first assignment is to chip the defensive end (DE) or Will on the left side. By 'chip,' I mean crush. The DE or Will is already being blocked by our left tackle (LT) and is, therefore, in a vulnerable, stand-up position. The HB's job is to crack the DE or Will in the ribs as hard as he can, which will impede the DE's or Will's ability to get around the LT and come after the quarterback (i.e., me). Then, after the 'chip,' the HB slides to the outside for the outlet.

Let me stop here for a second and summarize for the purpose of making an important point later. In *92 Lex Flanker Zid*, I have five possible receivers. Z is going deep. X and Y are going 18 and 12-14 yards downfield, respectively. My HB and FB are short, but they are my last resort. A play like this, that is designed principally for the intermediate and deep passing routes, and in which the short routes are available only in case of emergency, was considered basic and fundamental to the NFL style of play in my era. The intermediate and deep routes were my personal bread and butter.

As complicated as all these options may seem, there is one additional consideration which can muddy the waters even more. That's when the defense that you thought was your friendly *Weak Eagle Cover 4* turns out to be some kind of blitz. You always have to remember that the defense thinks, too; they're not just waiting around to see what you come up with. And a well-timed, well-executed blitz can throw a monkey wrench into everything I have just been describing.

Most of the time, I was pretty good at picking up the blitz. And very often, defenses give away the blitz. When safeties start creeping toward the line, for example, from their normal 14 yards to 10, then you know that life is about to happen very quickly for you. When the weak safety is not playing at the numbers (the yardage numbers painted on the field, which defensive backs use to space themselves), he may be cheating to the middle to cover for a strong safety who is planning to blitz. If the corners are playing a little soft, that also tells you something may be up. If the safeties are blitzing, the CB's have to be ready to defend everything beyond the scrum all by themselves, with no help in the center; so they play back a bit or they play heavy bump-and-run coverage.

But even if the DB's held their proper positions, sometimes I could just smell a blitz. If they're coming for you, there is a special, homicidal glint that you can often read in their eyes, and there's a sense you feel in your gut.

But I am not the Pope - I am not infallible. Sometimes I didn't know the blitz was coming until the ball was snapped. In those situations sight adjustments overrule anything that I may have called in the huddle or signaled at the line. When this happens the running backs try to pick up blitzers, and the receivers adjust according to the coverage (i.e., what they saw in front of them) hence 'sight adjustments.' If a corner was playing soft, the receiver would slant, knowing that I had maybe 1.2 or 1.3 seconds to make a three-step drop and get rid of the ball, which equates to maybe six yards downfield. On the other hand if a corner pressed, the receiver might go for the fade, or bomb, knowing that I could hit him up to 30 yards in 1.7 seconds (a five-step drop). In that case I would be flattened by the blitz, but I could get the pass off.

What does all this have to do with preparation? Well, as I mentioned in the last chapter, there are literally hundreds of plays like *92 Lex Flanker Zid* to master. And when I say 'master,' I don't mean just comprehend the theory of the play intellectually, like it was some kind of physics problem. I mean internalize it and practice it until it is burned into your muscle memory like a knee-jerk reflex. There is no time to think it over. Everything about *92 Lex Flanker Zid* that I just spent five pages describing (and I left out a lot of details, like line blocking assignments and flanker or running back motion before the set and various forms of sight adjustment) happens in less than three seconds. Say it: one Mississippi, two Mississippi, three Missi.... That leaves you no time for searching the memory banks. You just have to study it and drill it until it's second nature, like breathing. And you have to do it for several *hundred* play possibilities.

This is why, at least in my day, quarterbacks selected in the first round of the draft normally spent their rookie year standing on the sidelines charting plays. No matter where they went to college, no matter who their coaches had been, they weren't deemed ready for the NFL.

This was my fate, too. My initial job with the Browns was to understudy Gary Danielson, an established, 10-year NFL veteran, who also happened to be a great mentor. I am talking about the same Gary Danielson whom you probably know as the on-air commentator for CBS Sports. Such are his football smarts.

Anyway, Gary got hurt mid-season, so I had to step in. Until that happened, however, I was a highly paid spectator and occasional practice prop. Even though I had won a national championship. Even though I had had Howard Schnellenberger, Earl Morrall, Marc Trestman, Gary Stevens, and Jimmy Johnson for collegiate coaches, all NFL veterans running a pro-style offense at Miami.[9] Earl Morrall was the winning QB in two Super Bowls, for crying out loud. None of that mattered. Sorry, Bernie, you're not quite ready for prime time. Just watch and learn.

Believe me, I am not complaining. The apprenticeship tradition made a lot of sense to me, given all the preparation that is required. And that was back in my day when there were no regulatory limits on the amount of time that college athletes could devote to their game.

Nowadays, there's just no time in college athletics to learn everything you have to learn. Today, you are limited by NCAA rules to 20 hours a week of football activity. Shoot, there were times when I spent close to 20 hours a *day*. Twenty hours a week? And you can't cheat and try to cram in a few extra hours of watching film or lifting weights; you will be caught.

Of necessity, therefore, the college game is much simpler than the pro game. And this tendency is increasingly reinforced by other factors. One is the incredible athleticism of today's players. You get a specimen who is 6'5" and made of pure muscle, who runs the 40 in 4.3 seconds, and you don't need to get fancy. You just need to get the ball to him any way you can and let him outrun or overpower everybody else. Even in my day coaches regularly told me to get the ball to the real athlete, ASAP. Let the Big Dawg eat.

Another factor reinforcing the simplification of the college game is the big money that has come to dominate college football over the years. Division I coaches don't make professor pay anymore. Most of them are now pulling down millions of dollars a year (not counting endorsements

---

9 Fun fact: Gary is one of the few Irish guys I ever knew who grew up in Little Italy in Cleveland. And I believe I was the only guy to play with Jimmy Johnson at the U, the Dolphins, and the Cowboys.

and other outside income). For that kind of money, you are expected to win, and a lot of alumni donations are riding on these victories. You are not compensated to prep people for the NFL or dream up complex new schemes or experiment with novel approaches. You are paid to win, and the path of least resistance is to recruit that monster speed demon and just get him the ball. I don't criticize the coaches for doing this. If I were a college coach today, I would do the exact same thing.

Unfortunately, from my point of view, these developments, combined with the limited prep time in college, have produced a game with a lot of dinks and dunks; that is, a lot of short passes that anybody can throw. The intermediate and deep routes, like those I described in *92 Lex Flanker Zid* that are so basic and fundamental in the pro game, are growing increasingly rare in the college game. As a result collegiate quarterbacks are increasingly prized as much, or more, for their running ability as they are for their passing skills.

At the same time the dink-dunk passing game means that linemen don't have to hold blocks for three or four seconds, like my guys tried to do, because the ball is typically released in less than two seconds. Hell, they could all miss their blocks and it wouldn't matter. The ball is immediately out in the flats somewhere. Consequently, the linemen who are headed to the NFL to protect the quarterbacks aren't ready for prime time, either. So when you pluck a college quarterback out of that kind of system and parachute him directly into the NFL, it should come as no surprise that some of them will get slaughtered. Suffice it to say here that these young men are not prepared for the next level. They hardly know what the word 'preparation' means in the professional context.

This is a harsh lesson to learn for someone who has vaulted from the pee wee leagues all the way through a premier Division I college program on sheer physical talent. But when you get to the elite level, you discover that your phenomenal talent is no longer so extraordinary. At the top everybody is phenomenal. You are no longer the exception; you are now typical. Talent no longer separates you from the pack. At the pinnacle of your profession, the differentiators are now attitude, as described in Chapter 2, and preparation, as described here.

I might add, this isn't just football wisdom. It's true of any profession you choose. As Thomas Edison once said, "Opportunity is missed by most people because it is dressed up in overalls and looks like work."

Chapter 5
LEADERSHIP

Just because someone is charge of an organization, it doesn't mean he or she is a leader. In fact, if things are bad in an organization, it could be because there is no leadership. Leadership is a positive attribute. It either exists in an organization, or it doesn't. If it exists, the organization generally prospers. If it doesn't, the organization generally sucks, or to be more polite, it's an organization in name only. In reality, an organization without leadership is just a chaotic collection of individuals all looking out for their own selfish interests.

There is such a thing as a bad boss. We have all run into him or her. A bad boss is a person in a position of authority who is not a leader. So what's the difference between a boss and a leader? One simple answer is that people follow a boss because they have to, but they follow a leader because they want to. The leader applies positive motivations, like, "I will help you achieve more." The boss relies on negative sanctions, like, "I can fire you." By appealing to the positive, the leader can generate a belief in the group's potential and, thus, elicit what is known as 'discretionary effort' from his followers. The boss will mostly get the bare minimum. That discretionary effort is what sometimes separates the champions from the also-rans.

This is true in football, and especially true for quarterbacks. If all you get from your linemen and receivers is minimum effort, then you are going to get sacked a lot, and you are going to throw a lot of incompletions. Either way, your career will be short. I needed my linemen to hold blocks for four seconds, not two, because I liked to throw long, and I clearly wasn't going to scramble my way out of trouble while the receivers broke free. And my guys did it, eventually. Our first games of the season were often pretty ugly because guys didn't come out of training camp ready to hold blocks as long as I needed them to. But as the season progressed, and throughout the postseason, my teammates always came through largely because they bought into the program. You could argue they simply got into better playing shape as the season wore on, but I would remind you that they were also way more banged up. The difference, in my opinion, was discretionary effort and a shared belief that what we were doing was going to benefit everybody.

My own leadership style with the Browns was a quirky combination of factors. Off the field I did my best to be one of the guys. We went out together (and with our girlfriends, of course). We didn't have Facebook and Instagram in those days, but if we did, any picture you would have seen of me out on the town would have been with my teammates or family members. No entourage, no posse, just teammates. We played cards together (and I forgave a lot of poker debts). We busted balls together. I did my best to buddy up to everybody. I believed – and still do – that everyone is important because everyone contributes to the success of the team.

This was the approach I had used in college to win the support of my teammates. I have to confess that my early efforts at the camaraderie thing were a little sketchy. Part of it was my youth and inexperience. A lot of it had to do with the situation in Miami at that time.

This was not the glamorous Miami of South Beach and Coconut Grove that we know today. This was Miami of the early 80's, only a couple years after the Mariel boat lift, an exodus of some 10,000 Cubans who fled the Castro regime between April and October 1980, in all manner of boats. Included among the refugees were a considerable number of criminals and mental patients released from their respective institutions by Castro, to simplify his life and complicate ours.

This Miami was drug wholesaler to the eastern United States, if not all of North America. Vast ghettoes and barrios provided fertile recruiting territory for really, really tough guys to play football. But they also provided a clear and present danger to basic survival. We all carried guns in those days, not because we were macho show-offs, but because we all feared for our safety. I myself got shot at a couple of times. Luckily I wasn't seriously injured.

In this context some of my teammates thought nothing of a little petty crime, such as robbing pizza delivery guys on campus, in order to finance 'weekend money.' A couple of my teammates once robbed a pizza guy who happened to be a classmate of theirs. They didn't recognize him because they didn't go to class very much. But he recognized them because they were well-known members of the football team. As a result they were busted. So to save them from getting booted off the team, or out of school, or worse, I volunteered to the coach that I was a part of the whole thing. I calculated that the coach wouldn't throw his first-string quarterback off the team, and that it would go easier for my teammates if I were principally to blame.

The coach knew damn well that I had nothing to do with it (except for the fact that I did, admittedly, eat the pizza). But he also knew what I was up to, and he also didn't want to lose his players. So we were all sentenced to pay back the stolen money, and we were forced into the infamous "Breakfast Club." That meant we had to run exercises like the bear crawl the entire length of the football field back and forth from end zone to end zone for two hours every morning, starting at 4:45 AM. I was sentenced to less than a week, the others to a few months. My teammates all thought my intervention was a pretty stand-up thing to do, even if it were kind of whacky, and as a result, I had their allegiance. Proving that I was one of the guys and not some self-important diva was always key to establishing leadership with the team.

That was off the field. On the field it was similar in that I took accountability for mistakes. For instance, when a receiver ran the wrong route, I would take the blame publicly during the next film study. Privately, I would talk to him and straighten out the issue, but I think this helped me to build credibility with my teammates.

Inside the huddle, however, I was a ruthless dictator. Nobody spoke in my huddle but me. I was the Lord thy God, and thou shalt have no other gods before me. As the quarterback, I was taught to be the leader like this.

In my very first huddle as a Cleveland Brown, substituting for Gary Danielson after he hurt his shoulder, a player started to speak, and I screamed at him to pipe down. I then proceeded to fumble my very first snap as a Cleveland Brown. What a moron, huh? But after a few humiliating minutes on the sideline, practicing snaps while the fans hooted at me, I went in a second time, acted even crazier in the huddle, and then proceeded to complete 10 of my next 11 attempts. That tended to quiet the critics.

So why was I such an asshole in the huddle? Where did I get the balls, as a twenty-one-year-old rookie fresh out of college, to confront seasoned NFL veterans in my very first appearance? First of all, that's the way I was trained in college at the U. Schnellenberger, Morrall, Stevens, and Trestman beat into my brain that I was supposed to be the leader of the offense, and I had to take charge. I bought into that concept. I was determined to own the huddle. I would tell players, "It's not a democracy here, it's a dictatorship." In college, I threw guys out of the huddle a few times for not focusing on the play at hand. I don't have time to take questions from the audience. Shut up and do what I tell you. A few times in the pros, I actually ran plays with 10 guys because I had to kick someone out of the huddle.

Now, I grant you that being a huddle-Nazi sounds more like bossiness than leadership. Obviously, there's more to it. The rapport I established with the guys off the field, as noted before, was critical. But I also had to deliver the goods. Had I continued to fumble snaps, my career would have been extremely short. The key, in that first game, was all the completions I managed, plus, of course, the victory. I had to perform. Once I did, then teammates started to buy in, and I was on my way.

Leadership results from your teammates believing that your way works. You can't just order them around. You have to show that your orders produce success – for the entire team.

My teammates generally bought into the program. The coaches, not so much. Once again, my college mentors had trained me to call my own plays. The Schnellenberger/Morrall/Trestman/Stevens theory was that, as quarterback, I was the last guy to read the defense before the snap. Therefore, I was the logical guy to determine what play to run against the particular defense in front of me. That theory won a national championship with a previously unheralded team, so it made a lot of sense to me.

My Browns coaches didn't share that theory. Bud Carson and Marty Shottenheimer and Lindy Infante all believed that my job was to run the plays they called. They were the coaches. They had studied the film, they had developed the game plans, they had the spotters up in the booth. Furthermore, they were the bosses. Although we had heated discussions, I learned over time that as long as I had facts to back up my ideas, and I was creating positive results, we all ended up winning.

I already mentioned how I would draw up my own play lists for every game when I thought I could add something. For example, the coaches always wanted to pull Ozzie Newsome on third down passing situations. Excuse me? Ozzie Newsome – one of the great tight ends of all time? Having the tight end in created more options, so I would keep Oz in the play so he could possibly block on a blitz, or be my leak-out. I would also improvise and send Reggie Langhorne deep. Reggie would fret, "They'll cut me!" I had to assure them both that I would take the heat. And I did. That's part of being a leader.

So the coaches would carp at me at times for my calls, and I would consider their ideas and do what I thought would work. What were they going to do? Bench me? I drive the team for a touchdown, and they're going to bench me because I didn't follow orders? It was an interesting lesson in leadership. You may be the boss, but if my play-calling produces the desired result, who's really the leader here? Is it the players? The coaches? The front office suits? It seems to me that as of late, front offices have been the focus of NFL team leadership.

Just look at my poor Brownies. They haven't won a championship since the Paul Brown era. The last Browns championship was in 1964 under head coach Blanton Collier, who had been Paul Brown's assistant before Brown was fired by owner Art Modell in 1963. Since my era they have rarely even been competitive. Since the 'new' Browns were established in 1998, playing their first season in 1999, through the 2016 season, they have had exactly two winning seasons. In the other 16 years during that period, their combined record was 68-159, a winning percentage below .300. How is it possible, you might ask, to be consistently that bad?

I'm not sure what image to go with here. Snake pit? Crabs in a barrel? For too long too many people in the Browns front office have not demonstrated what I think is part of a winning culture of leadership. It seems that for so long, they have not been committed to winning with every breath they take. It's easy to talk about winning, but much harder to do. It's often great to have football people who actually may have played the game at the highest level. Consider the success my buddy Ozzie Newsome[10] has had as General Manager in Baltimore, or John Elway as Denver's GM. Or they may have been coaches with a gift for comprehending absolutely everything that happens on the field and who also possess the smarts to

---

10 Early in the Al Lerner era, I recommended Ozzie for the GM position on the Browns, as well as Bill Belichick for head coach. Carmen Policy laughed at me and said, "Ozzie is a scout, and Belichick is horrible for marketing."

identify what's not working. Perhaps most important, they possess the self-confidence to admit this (at least to themselves) and fix it. Of the coaches I have worked with, I'm talking about Schnellenberger, Shula, Johnson, Belichick, Schottenheimer – that's what Cleveland needs, or any team, for that matter – people who know what it takes to win on the field and are committed to the view that "winning is the only thing."

Instead, Cleveland too often has had a parade of front-office suits with no on-field resumes (much less winning ones) who are into being big-shot executives. For so long, especially at the beginning of the new era, their game seemed to focus on staying in power and hanging on to their lucrative salaries and fancy perks, hobnobbing with the billionaire owner and his people, and generally appearing important. The talents required to achieve those goals have nothing to do with winning football games and nothing to do with leadership. The talent needed for the 'me-first' game is the talent for icing out competition that might vie for the attention of the owner, the media, the fans, or the underlings.

I myself have been iced out a few times. Carmen Policy told me to my face that he was going to take the 5% ownership stake I was supposed to have in the Browns when Al Lerner was owner (at least Policy was honest about it, but more about this incident in Chapter 9). In addition, Alec Scheiner, then President of the Browns, got me booted off radio shows and TV broadcasts of Browns games. As a result, I made a personal apology to him for whatever offenses he thought I may have committed and stressed my loyalty to the Browns organization. Scheiner tweeted my apology all over the planet but then continued to freeze me out. In March 2016, I am not at all sad to report, Scheiner left the Browns organization for reasons that were never made public.

I guess I was too critical of play calling, draft strategy, game plans – you know, the things that win football games. If your personal game plan is to suppress criticism and avoid blame that might cost you your precious job, you have to take steps against people who might know better.

This type of attitude leads to a downward spiral. When the team loses, somebody has to take the fall, other than the people who are supposed to be in charge. So they fire the coach, or the GM, or both. Now the team has a new coach working with players he didn't help draft. Or it has a GM working with coaches he had no say in selecting, or vice versa. It's a formula for chaos, not teamwork – for bosses, not leadership.

Then, once it becomes common knowledge that the average lifespan of a Browns head coach is two years (maybe), who would want that job? Certainly not anyone with Super Bowl ambitions. As a result, either the team is forced to settle for somebody's assistant coach who is willing to do some hard time to build his resume, or a coach who is willing to endure a couple brutal years in exchange for a five-year, multi-million dollar contract. In other words suffer for two years, hit the beach for three. Or double-dip with another team, collecting a paycheck from them as well as the Browns for the three years still left on your old Cleveland contract.

So what's the bottom line here? Leadership is not about authority that is given to you from on high, nor is it about your rank or how much power you are allowed to wield over others. Leadership is about commitment to the collective goal. If you are constantly thinking about how much you can grab for yourself, or how to duck blame for your mistakes, or whether people will think you're a big shot, well then, you probably will never be more than a boss, and most likely, less.

But if you put the collective goal above your personal self-interest, you have a shot at being a good leader. That may mean withstanding more criticism and punishment than anybody else in order to prove your commitment to the goal. That may mean taking blame, not only for your own screw-ups but for failures of the group as well in order to prove your commitment to the team. Leadership entails a lot of painful, personal sacrifice. But if you want to be a leader, it has to be all about the group, not you.

Chapter 6
DISCIPLINE

Itouch on the subject of discipline throughout this book, such as the discipline to do *exactly* what I tell you in the huddle, or the discipline to behave yourself 24/7, off the field as well as on, in the interest of focusing on victory. But there is an irony embedded in the concept of discipline that I'd like to examine as well.

The irony is that sometimes discipline can actually be liberating. To explain this, I first have to show you a page entitled "Training Camp Schedule" from an old Browns manual:

6:45 A.M.	WAKE UP CALLS
7:00 A.M.	BREAKFAST (ALL PLAYERS MUST SIGN IN)
8:40 A.M.	SPECIAL TEAMS (ON FIELD)
	POSITION MEETINGS FOR PLAYERS NOT INVOLVED
	WITH SPECIAL TEAMS
9:00 A.M.	PRACTICE BEGINS
11:15 A.M.	PRACTICE ENDS
11:20 A.M.	WEIGHTS (BY POSITION)
12:00 P.M.	LUNCH
12:45 P.M.	"SIESTA"
2:45 P.M.	PRE-PRACTICE
3:00 P.M.	PRACTICE BEGINS
5:15 P.M.	PRACTICE ENDS
5:20 P.M.	WEIGHTS (BY POSITION)
6:00 P.M.	DINNER
7:00 P.M.	SPECIAL TEAMS MEETING
7:30 P.M.	GENERAL TEAM MEETING
10:00 P.M.	COACHES MEETING
11:00 P.M.	BED CHECK (ALL PLAYERS IN THEIR OWN ROOMS)

Now *that's* discipline. Your entire day from wake-up call to bed check is mapped out for you in increments from one to five minutes. And when it says pre-practice begins at 2:45 PM, it doesn't mean 2:46. There will be an ear-shattering whistle or horn at exactly 2:45, and if you're not there, if you're still trotting out of the locker room or chatting up friends, there will be consequences both physically and financially. Violators in my day were sentenced to 'Breakfast Club,' which started at 4:45 A.M., and consisted of punishing physical drills like the bear crawl for two hours *before* you reported to actual breakfast. Not only were the drills excruciating, but the coaches who had to supervise Breakfast Club stayed mad at you for a long time because they didn't want to be up at that hour either.

To free-spirited individuals, such tight regimentation might sound horrifying. It's the complete opposite of freedom. It's what you imagine life in prison must be like.

Yes and no. It's true, we weren't free to do what we pleased when we wanted to. But I actually appreciated the regimentation. I liked not having to make decisions about what I was going to do all day. Lord knows, I had enough brain strain going on, trying to master all the plays, trying to remember everything I had studied about opponents, and trying to figure out how to deal with the capabilities and tendencies of my individual teammates.

In season we weren't as regimented as we were in training camp, where we were all living together like boot camp recruits. In season we were allowed to go home at night and have a little privacy. But the week was still pretty structured. Monday, we were supposed to report bright and early for work-outs. In theory we had Tuesdays off, but as noted earlier, I spent my Tuesdays studying film and getting physical therapy (hopefully simultaneously to maximize my time). Wednesdays we got the game plan and worked on first and second down plays for the upcoming opponent. Thursdays, we worked on third down plays. Fridays, we worked on Red Zone plays (i.e., offense within 20 yards of the opponent's goal). On Saturdays we would rehearse some more. So there was not a lot of free time in the regular season either.

I also appreciated this. Most of the time I was not on the field, I was watching film and cooking up the game plan. I had billions of decisions to make. What is our opponent likely to do in any of a few hundred situations, and what was I going to do about it? Figuring all that out during weekly preparation was hard enough. On game day I now had to make all these decisions at hyper-speed, in the fog of war, with enormous wild beasts chasing me around, trying to kill me. I had a very full diet of decision-making. I didn't crave more. I was grateful not to have to think about what I was supposed to do or where I was supposed to be at any given moment. It was a relief, actually. It allowed me to focus on what was really important to me, namely, winning games, without getting distracted by time management issues. So the discipline of football, as least as it related to my personal schedule, actually liberated me to do my job better.

Discipline can also be considered roughly comparable to the law. The law represents the social discipline that we are all supposed to observe for the collective good of society. So a disciplined person must also be a law-abiding citizen, right?

No doubt, in general civilian life, that is a true statement. But it doesn't necessarily hold true on the football field. Clearly, there are a lot of rules in football, and players know what they are. However, that doesn't stop them from trying to get away with whatever the hell they can. Their job is to win, and most players are willing to do so by whatever means necessary. So players rarely ask themselves, "Am I doing something illegal?" They know damn well when they're doing something illegal. Their main question is, "Will I get caught?"[11] That was one of the basic principles of my playing philosophy. If the ref didn't throw a flag, it wasn't illegal. No flag, no foul. I could poke out your eye in the pile or chew off your finger, but if it didn't draw a flag, then it wasn't illegal. It's kind of like being a defendant in a criminal trial. It's not the defendant's job to prove he didn't do it; it's the government's job to prove that he did. That's why when defendants get off, we don't say they're innocent. We say they are 'not guilty.' Big difference.

At the same time being a habitual offender equates to a lack of discipline, in my view. The 'anything goes' mentality only works as long as you don't get flagged. If you're generating penalties left and right, you're hurting the team. So you have to be cagey. We all know, for example,

---

11 My friend and teammate, three-time Pro Bowl cornerback Hanford Dixon, will tell you in an honest moment that he held receivers if he had to. Old-timers will recall that Hanford was the originator, along with fellow cornerback Frank Minnifield, of the 'Dawg' phenomenon for which Cleveland is now famous. Check it out in his book, Day of the Dawg (Gray & Co.: 2012).

that the instigator doesn't draw the flag, the retaliator does. You can shove some guy in the back when everybody's attention is on the other side of the field where the play is. But if somebody shoves you in the back, you have to resist the temptation to shove him in return, because it's likely that everybody will witness that, and the yellow hankies will come flying out all over. Believe me, that restraint takes discipline.

The final point about discipline goes to the very essence of football: how do players manage to control themselves? To understand what I mean by 'control,' you need to understand the mental attitude that is required to win football games at the highest level, which I can sum up in one word: homicidal. Or maybe two words: violently homicidal. Or maybe six words: unthinkably, savagely, remorselessly, and violently homicidal.

You could be my best friend in the world, but if you were on the opposing team, I would be ready and willing to do anything to win, especially if you were a friend. I had to have that mindset. I would not give it a second thought. No hesitation, no reservations, and no regrets whatsoever. That's how bad I wanted to win games.

That may sound frightening, but it's the truth. Recall Chapter 2 on *attitude*. You get so cranked up to win the game that you would kill for it – on the field.

Off the field, of course, you have to behave like a normal, law-abiding citizen. You have to leave the homicidal attitude in the locker room with your helmet and your cleats. Not an easy transition. You're supposed to be like a light switch – power on, power off. But it's really hard to do. So what's the secret? How do players do it?

A good analogy is police dogs, or army attack dogs. When they have their collars on, they are happy, lovable, over-sized puppies. Kids can hug them around the neck, and they just sit there, wagging their tails, and drinking in the love. But when the handler takes off the collar, these same dogs turn into vicious, unstoppable beasts. Finally, after they have brought down their target and the handler slips the collar back on, they are happy, lovable, over-sized puppies again.

People aren't dogs, though (except in Browns Town, where they are 'dawgs'). People can't effortlessly toggle between homicide and serenity.

While humanity's warrior instincts are still within each of us, they are buried deep in the psyche under centuries of civilizing behavior. Consequently, it takes a disciplined, conscious effort to dredge them up for a few hours of combat and then, even more important, bury them back deep in the soul when the combat is over, so that nobody gets hurt or killed.

There is no specific formula for accomplishing this. Every player has his own personal technique. You have seen film of pre-game locker rooms. One player is sitting motionless on a bench, as if in prayer, or at least in deep thought. Another player is banging his head against lockers. Two other guys are shoving each other into an enraged state. Everybody has his own individual approach to the pre-game psych-up.

My own method involved a combination of techniques. One was prayer, though not of a particularly pious variety. I wasn't praying for forgiveness or wisdom or humility or even protection – those virtuous things you are supposed to pray for. Again, in retrospect, if I'm being honest with myself, I was probably trying to cut a deal with the Lord to cover all my bases. O Lord, I would pray, if we win, I will give a bunch of money to charity, or be good for a year, or give up sex. Whatever I thought would appeal to the Lord (and make me feel comfortable in what I was trying to do) as an attractive bargain, I would offer that up in exchange for a 'W.' Please don't tell my parish priest.

A more important part of my routine was what I call aggressive silence. Starting maybe 18 hours before game time, no more chit-chat, no more ball-busting, in fact, no more human interaction, except with players and coaches. Just me and the play lists I had been working on all week. Thinking, re-thinking, visualizing in my mind how the plays would develop. Gradually, hour by hour, this mental drilling would concentrate my psyche into game-level intensity.

A third part of my routine, once we were in the locker room on game day, was prepping my teammates. "Web, watch for the gun," (my hand signal for a double move deep throw) or "Reg, we're doing the 50 Double Seam versus a Cover 2. Alert the middle read." In other words, I would inform them of key plays I wanted to run and get *them* mentally rehearsing their roles in order to help prepare them. Receivers might run 15 or 20 routes in a game without ever touching the ball. It helps them keep their focus when they know they are going to get their chances. And as they got psyched up, their rising intensity level helped feed my own. By the time we charged out of the tunnel, I was ready for war.

Then, after the game, it was necessary to dial it all back and return to normal. This, too, is a process. To reiterate, you can't just flick a switch like you're turning the lights on and off. Tony Dungy and Bill Polian[12] used to tell me that there should be a 24-hour, post-game cool-down period for players. You can't just walk out of the killing zone and immediately act happy-go-lucky. I sometimes wonder if the media guys who stick microphones in players' mouths five minutes after a painful loss realize how close they are flirting with death. For me it took every bit of a full day to chill out after a loss.

But even after a win, there is a process. You can't afford to spend any time celebrating. If you spend too much time congratulating yourself, you run the risk of complacency. I had to try to forget about a win even faster than I had to try to forget about a loss. I had to put that out of my mind and start thinking about next week.

Not all players had a mechanism for dialing it up and dialing it down. Some guys just had a permanent mean streak. They were flat-out vicious all the time. Every good team I was involved with always had four to six of them. You needed to have a few merciless killers on the squad in order to create and maintain that physical dominance of your team. But four to six was the limit because you had to watch these guys 24/7 off the field to make sure they didn't kill anyone in a brawl at a night club, or manhandle a waiter because the steak was too well-done, or pull out a gun in a fit of road rage. If you had 10 or 12 of these types, well, there just wouldn't be enough 'sane' players left on the roster to babysit all the tough guys around the clock. So four to six was the definite limit.

And yet, I learned something from these rough guys, particularly the ones I first encountered in college on the tough streets of Mariel-Boat-Lift Miami. I thought I grew up tough in Youngstown. Friday night rumbles with high school archrivals were routine. No sissy boys in Youngstown. But we had nothing on *real* bad boys from extremely violent neighborhoods. You might get a bloody nose in one of our Friday night rumbles, or a nasty bruise, or maybe even a broken arm. But we

---

12 Tony Dungy, now an NBC analyst, was head coach of the Tampa Bay Buccaneers and the Indianapolis Colts, and between the two teams, he set a record for most consecutive playoff appearances as a coach (10). Tony was inducted into the NFL Hall of Fame in 2016. Bill Polian, now an ESPN analyst, was an executive with several teams, most notably the Buffalo Bills, who made a record four straight Super Bowl appearances while he was general manager.

didn't have people spraying AK gunfire off of I-680 in Ohio the way they did off of U.S. 1 in Florida. We didn't have gang-style executions or rampant drug trafficking. There was no real law where these guys came from, except maybe the Law of the Street.

So being around them toughened me up, no doubt about it. I learned about a world where everything is a confrontation. If you back down, even from the slightest, pettiest indignity, you will be bullied to death, maybe literally.

The difference between them and me was that confrontation was an acquired skill for me, and it became necessary for my survival. It was a skill that came in very handy, and in fact, was indispensable on the gridiron. But after the game I could go back to normal, given a little time. For the tough guys I'm talking about, crazy, violent confrontation *was* normal.

I suppose you could put it down to upbringing. Tough as Youngstown may have been compared to some comfy suburban community, there was still some discipline in my youth. I was an altar boy in church. I went to Catholic schools until high school. I at least knew the difference between right and wrong, even if I didn't always respect it. Guys from the truly brutal neighborhoods had no such point of reference. In their world the choices were fight or die.

There is a theme that unites all these various points about discipline. In some ways discipline is the diametric opposite of freedom, which we all cherish as Americans, and which we have fought wars to protect. And yet you have to have discipline to achieve certain objectives, ranging from avoiding penalty flags to winning Super Bowls. This form of discipline – self-discipline – requires limits on individual freedom to achieve some greater good. Self-discipline is not to be confused with discipline imposed from the outside, otherwise known as punishment. Obviously, you want to avoid that kind of discipline if at all possible.

There is a lesson in all this for up-and-coming young athletes. In our culture, it is easy for elite athletes to believe they can get away with just about anything. In high school and college, they are coddled by coaches who will go to extreme measures to keep them on their team. Discipline issues are often overlooked, academic issues sometimes negotiated, attitude problems mostly tolerated. There are often very few consequences for bad behavior. So many young athletes grow up thinking that their gifts elevate them above the rules that ordinary people have to follow. They believe they are free to do whatever they please. My message to these young stars is simple: learn to discipline yourself – before someone does it for you.

Not too long ago, the Browns suffered through a painful example of this lesson in the sorry case of Johnny Manziel. The Browns, not known in recent years for their great success in the draft, used their first round pick in 2014 to select Manziel from Texas A&M, where he had earned the moniker 'Johnny Football' for his flamboyant style of play. But his 'flamboyance' extended beyond the playing field and caused major personal and legal problems. The upshot was that he accomplished very little in two seasons with the Browns. I sure wish the Browns had let me talk to Johnny when they first drafted him.

Chapter 7
BROTHERHOOD

In my day ball-busting was a time-honored tradition in the locker room. Ball-busting (or verbal hazing) covered a broad range of insults that took many different forms. The tamest was the nickname. If you had any distinguishing physical features at all, players would re-name you Dumbo (for big ears) or Cue Ball (for baldness) or Needle Dick (for, well, you know).

At the next level ball-busts would insult you more directly, as in "You're so ugly, I bet your mamma used to tie pork chops to your ears so the dogs would play with you," or "You're so dumb you couldn't find your own asshole with both hands and a flashlight."

Maybe you're laughing, right? Maybe you're disgusted. This stuff can be funny, at least for most guys. While I never enjoyed it, ball-busting is a reality, especially in the NFL. Women insult each other, too, but I think they usually mean it. They're not clowning around; they're doing battle.

While it might seem insulting to some, ball-busting, at least back then in the NFL, could be reassuring. For reasons I'll explain shortly, ball-busting could build camaraderie and brotherhood. Once you got used to ball-busting as the normal mode of interaction, you realized that it meant you were considered one of the guys. On the other hand, when everybody started acting nice and polite, you started to worry because that was not normal. It meant that you were possibly not one of the guys anymore and that a trade or release might be imminent. It's sort of like what Tom Hanks said about his men in *Saving Private Ryan*: "I don't worry about them griping all the time. I worry when they stop griping."

The most extreme form of ball-busting was when guys described sex acts they had performed with the women in your life – wife, girlfriend, mother, sister – and how much those women enjoyed it. In any other context these kinds of ball-busts would have started an instant fistfight, but in the locker room (and on the field), they were commonplace and accepted.

The ball-bust served several purposes. In the first place it functioned as a tentative expression of friendship, believe it or not. For example, if I gave you a nickname that mocked some aspect of your anatomy, it meant that you were part of the family or team. It meant that I thought you would take it in the right way and not go ballistic on me.

In that regard the ball-bust was also a test. If you took it the wrong way and got all crazy on me, well then, maybe you weren't really a part of the family. It was also a test in another sense. If I insulted you, it implied that I was not worried about what you might do to me in response. It meant I did not fear you. In that sense the ball-bust was a challenge: Do you think you're tougher than me? I don't.

But more important, we ball-busted primarily to build camaraderie. Whatever went on in the locker room was designed to tighten our bonds so we would know that when we stepped onto the field we had each other's backs. Ball-busting did sometimes serve as a test for younger players, because if they couldn't handle something minor – insults – then how were they going to respond in the fourth quarter with all the challenges and the chaos around them?

I give you this analysis of ball-busting as background for a story that still puzzles me to this day. It is a story that raises questions about the fuzzy lines between brotherhood and ball-busting and outright viciousness, and it reveals something about how the game has changed since I played. I am referring here to the well-publicized confrontation between Richie Incognito and Jonathan Martin, both offensive linemen for the Miami Dolphins in 2012 and 2013.

As many fans know, Incognito was suspended in 2013 for harassing his teammate Martin in a variety of ways – face to face, as well as via social media, phone calls, and voice mails. You can find the text of a lot of Incognito's messages on the Internet. They include racial slurs and all kinds of insults and obscenities directed at him as well as at his family members. In addition Incognito made physical threats and even death threats. The matter came to a head when Martin quit the team in late October 2013, eight games into the season, citing 'emotional reasons.' The Dolphins launched an immediate investigation which culminated in Incognito's suspension a week later.

I never met Incognito, but his resume suggests he was one of those 'permanent mean streak' guys I mentioned in the last chapter. He had a history of behavior issues that extended at least back to college.

As a member of the Miami Dolphins, Incognito took to abusing one of his own teammates. You might justifiably wonder why. Where's the brotherhood in that?

Like I said before, ball-busting is, to some degree, a training exercise intended to toughen up a player. Some of the reports of the Incognito/Martin episode suggest that Incognito's abuse was tolerated and perhaps even encouraged by the coaching staff for that very reason. I don't know if that's true or not, but in my day, it wouldn't have been at all surprising. Martin was not the first player, nor will he be the last, to be subjected to abuse intended to reveal whether or not he might be a 'soft' player. I yelled at teammates myself, often with very colorful language, when I thought their attitude or their lack of effort was hurting the cause.

If this Incognito business had taken place in any other work place, all my sympathies would be with Martin. But it took place in the NFL, which is not like any other work place, which leaves me with some confusion about Martin.

In the first place, I don't understand how you can even get into the NFL if you're at all sensitive to verbal abuse. Like I said before, the atmosphere of a football locker room contains more foul language than oxygen.

Throughout my own career one of the lessons that my best coaches hammered into my brain was, "Just do your job." Forget about distractions in your personal life. Just do your job. Forget about distractions on the field. Just do your job. Forget about pain and nagging injuries. Just do your job, as best you can. Insults and verbal abuse? Are you kidding me? Do your job. If hurt feelings can keep you from doing your job, what are you doing here?

As a quarterback I have particular concerns with an offensive lineman who is that susceptible to head games. Offensive linemen are supposed to protect quarterbacks. If my lineman isn't focused on his job because someone called him a pussy or whatever, then my own safety and well-being is in jeopardy (as is our collective ability to succeed). Do your job, man, or I could be killed. Worse yet, we could lose, and then you'd be letting down the entire team. All the rest of us are trying to win games here. You need to focus on blocking for *us*, your team, your brothers.

In total Martin played for three teams, sort of, in a theoretical four-year career. After his walk-out from the Dolphins in 2013, Miami traded him to San Francisco for a seventh round draft pick on condition that he make the Niners' roster. Martin started the first game of the 2014 season and then basically rode the bench until he was released on waivers the following spring. The Carolina Panthers picked him up, but he retired before the 2015 season began. I don't mean to be unsympathetic, but it seems that this guy was a disappointment to a lot of teammates on three different squads. Maybe he just wasn't cut out for the NFL. But, let's be fair – most people aren't cut out for the NFL.

Among other things, this saga shows how the times have changed since my day, and it reveals that we may have found that out-of-bounds marker I talked about earlier. In my era this whole incident would never have seen the light of day. Everything would have been handled 'in the family,' so to speak. But Incognito's taunts were not limited to the confines of the locker room. They were blasted all over the Internet in the form of tweets, text messages, and voice mail recordings. The whole world knew what was going on within days of Martin's departure from the Dolphins. The whole world got to peek inside an NFL locker room, and by the standards of the civilized world, what they saw was outrageous and intolerable.

People can debate whether social media is a blessing or a curse. Personally, I use it all the time myself. It's a great way to stay in touch with the fans, to announce public appearances, to promote causes I believe in, and things like that. I currently have almost 100,000 Twitter followers, and climbing. At the same time it's also a great platform for Bernie-bashers to vent all kinds of vicious, obscene, and ignorant opinions about me; so there's a downside as well. Regardless, it's here to stay, and the Incognito/Martin case may have a revolutionary impact on professional football. The social media storm over this incident may have redefined behavioral norms for the entire NFL. Whatever may have been condoned in the past and swept under the carpet is now subject to the bright light of public scrutiny. The football fraternity may not be able to enforce its own secret code of conduct anymore. The general public now has a say.

What does all this have to do with brotherhood? While I accept the general proposition that sunlight is the best disinfectant, I wonder about the effect of all this public disclosure on the game itself. More specifically, what will be the effect on the fraternity of players that is forged in the outrageous exchanges of the locker room? Will players just get a little cagier about how they test their teammates with ball-busts? Or will they tone it down a little bit? If you accept my theory that ball-busts are a way to test and to strengthen mental toughness, will dialing them back hinder a coach's ability to gauge the level of this important quality in a player? This is a critical determination since, in my view, mental toughness is every bit as important as physical ability.

Furthermore, if the locker room and the practice field become more genteel and politically correct, will the camaraderie among players be as strong? Can I be as confident of your performance if I don't know whether an opponent can get into your head? Can we be as friendly if I have to stop and think before I crack a joke? Will we have as much fun together if we always have to watch what we say, and where we say it?

I probably sound like one of those old-timers who growl about how football is getting sissified with too many rules and constraints. But ball-busting is different. I'm OK with rules against spearing the chin with the helmet, or roll-blocking knees, or (for sure) dismembering the quarterback after he has released the ball. Those are safety issues. But ball-busting is different. People generally don't wind up in the trainer's room or the hospital because of a ball-bust.[13]

I'm from a generation that believes that ball-busting strengthens the group. It is the language of brotherhood. It is how we exchange viewpoints frankly, to say the least, and without beating around the bush. It is how we express friendship without sounding mushy or sentimental. It may be crude, sexist, barbaric, unfiltered, and offensive to the extreme. But it is how we prepare ourselves collectively for the fierce business we have to do in the NFL.

I recognize that times have changed, and I hope that our newfound public scrutiny of off-the-field conduct will prevent another Incognito/Martin situation from ever happening again. But I also hope that it doesn't do too much damage to the fraternity of players. I will always believe that ball-busting builds brotherhood, and that brotherhood, in football as in other facets of life, is what builds a team.

---

13 People can, however, when this mental testing becomes more physical. For example, I ended up in the trainer's room after Doug Flutie's famous "Hail Mary" pass to Gerard Phelan, a play that knocked us out of national championship consideration in 1984. We were so disgusted by losing that game that the next day, a group of us went to the beach to play "Kill Frisbee." There were no rules, no penalties. I didn't think I needed further physical testing, since I had thrown for almost 500 yards in the game. Julio, Flemco, and Swampman (you all know who you are) had other ideas. If the game the day before were not brutal enough, they gave me a cracked jaw and a broken nose during "Kill Frisbee." I ended up going to the trainers that day and telling them it happened during the game against Boston College. Ball-busting that day led to more physical contact than usual, but I think I passed the test because I never complained or blamed anyone for it.

Chapter 8
MONEY: PART I - THE RISE

You know I made a lot of money in football. Compared to today's NFL scale, it might not seem so impressive. But even today, much less in 1985, a college graduate getting a contract north of a million dollars a year in his first gig out of school would be doing a happy dance all day long.

You may not know that I made even more money outside of football, mostly after I retired. I was involved in several companies that got really big really fast, and sold for really big bucks. I found myself doing deals with the likes of Barry Diller (InterActiveCorp) and Wayne Huizenga (Miami Dolphins owner) and Fox Sports along with a number of big-time private equity firms.

On the other hand, if you have seen the ESPN special, *Broke*, then you also know I filed for bankruptcy in 2009. I know this sounds like another "The Rise and Fall of the Dumb Jock" story that, unfortunately, has become so common it is practically cliché. I guarantee you that my story is not a cliché. I am going to relate it here for a couple reasons.

First of all, the sheer entertainment value of my story is worth the read. It is so bizarre that it borders on the incredible, even for me, even now. But my story makes a more important point about adversity. Everyone can relate to the stress and anxiety of falling behind on credit card payments, or medical bills, or, God help you, your taxes. Once you hear my saga, you will experience that pressure cranked up to a million pounds per square inch. But before we get into that, let me give you a brief summary of The Rise.

For openers I was not your stereotypical 'dumb jock.' Remember that I graduated from college with a major in finance and economics, in two and a half years. So I knew something about money and business from the get-go. I have always been very good with numbers and have never needed a calculator. Financial illiteracy was not my problem.

Fairly early in my pro career, I discovered that I could hold my own in negotiations with actual business people. When I first got into the League, the standard NFL contract had a clause that said a player did not own the rights to his own name. I don't own my own name? No: the NFL and the Browns had the rights to both my name and likeness. For example, they could market a product called, let's say, Kosar Cologne, and I had no rights to anything – not the product, not the profit, not a thing. It didn't even matter if I hated the product or didn't use cologne (which I don't). They could slap my name on anything and do what they wanted with it. And it wasn't just the Browns – it was League-wide. Individual players had minimal to no marketing rights to anything.

The union, that is, the National Football League Players Association (NFLPA) had some rights. But the NFLPA was kind of soft in those days, as compared to, say, the Major League Baseball Players Association, and what rights it did have were used to raise money for the union itself, not to benefit most players.

I considered this bullshit. Aside from the philosophical problem of owners owning our names, they weren't doing squat, as a practical matter, to market us, either for their own benefit or for anybody else's. So the first time I negotiated my own contract in 1987, I just drew a great big 'X' through that whole *Paragraph 5* clause.

I also shared my views with my fellow QB's around the League and found that a lot of them agreed with me. So in 1991, we formed the Quarterback Club (QBC) and went to town.[14] At our high point we had over 40 active members, and in 11 years, we passed out over $100 million to over 60 players. In 2002, we sold QBC to the players' union.

I have taken some crap over the years from various quarters about QBC. Nobody disputes our success. The main thrust of the criticism has been that QBC was a 'cartel' of a small minority of big-name players who made all the money, while the vast majority of players received nothing from the organization. I respond to this in two ways. First, it doesn't make any sense to try to market unknown players. The quarterbacks and a few other popular players who joined QBC had the public recognition that advertisers seek. How else were we supposed to do it?

---

14 The original members of QBC were me, Troy Aikman, Bubby Brister, Randall Cunningham, John Elway, Boomer Esiason, Jim Everett, Jim Kelly, Dan Marino, Warren Moon, Phil Simms, and Steve Young.

But my greater point is that QBC was instrumental in getting *all* players a better deal. In essence our success shamed the union into taking player marketing seriously. In 1994, after the NFLPA saw how well we were doing, they fired up Players Inc. to do the same thing we were doing, but for the membership at large. Eventually, they were able to ramp up Players Inc. to the point that it made sense to acquire QBC from us and roll everything into one big package. As of that acquisition, the NFLPA had paid out a quarter billion dollars, if not more, to players, as opposed to zero before QBC, and I'm sure they have paid out hundreds of millions more since then. So, in my opinion, all the beneficiaries of that money earned from player licensing deals owe a debt of gratitude to the Quarterback Club for leading the way.

I got involved in my first big, non-football deal while I was still in the League. I had a neighbor in Florida by the name of David Epstein, whom history has shown to be a business genius. David had started a company called Precision Response Corporation (PRC), which was a customer service call center with about 100 employees at the time.

This call center was a little different from the call centers of today. In the late 90's, when the Internet was just getting off the ground, websites were not as easy to navigate as they are now. Something like 80% of all attempted web purchases failed because users couldn't figure out how the sites worked. So we at PRC put a 'Help' button on the screen that would alert the call center. Someone at the call center could then contact the caller to help him or her navigate the computer screen in order to complete the transaction. Imagine: a help center that called *you*, not the other way around, and from America to boot.

I originally joined PRC as an advisor, but they soon made me a Director and Senior Vice-President. The company grew so fast that we became the fifth-largest employer in Miami, with 11,000 people. It was successful enough to attract the attention of Barry Diller, Chairman of InterActiveCorp, parent of USA Network, Home Shopping Network, Expedia.com, Match.com, and on and on. In 2000, Diller bought PRC for $728 million. We had some debt to pay off, but even after that, we netted $564 million, pre-tax. I had bought about 10% of PRC, holding it within a few different companies, before Diller came along. Do the math.[15]

---

15 David Epstein and I donated a chunk of our profits to the University of Miami. The University kindly named a new building at the business school in our honor.

In the late 90's, while I was still involved in PRC, I also helped to found a company called Wild Card Systems for about $1 million, and I became a Director on its board. The genius behind Wild Card was Larry Park, and he teamed up with another friend, Carl Pascarella, CEO of Visa, to develop and market a brilliant product called Visa Buxx. Visa Buxx was a debit, or 'stored value' card for teens, which allowed parents to load, monitor, and approve their children's purchases. This idea was so radical for the time that people close to me pressed for an intervention, fearing I had really gone crazy this time. Soon, however, others saw the value of this concept, and in 2005, we sold Wild Card Systems to E Funds for $228 million. My share equated to about $15 million.

Shortly after the sale of PRC, I helped found a Cleveland-based company called Envision Pharmaceutical Services, a benefits management company for pharmacies and mail-order drugs. I was on the Board of Directors, helped with the marketing and sales, and at one point, owned 10% of the company. That one sold in 2013 for $1 billion to a private equity firm, which turned around and sold it to Rite Aid in 2015 for $2 billion.

In 2001, I, along with people from Rivals.com bought into a website called Citadel.com and re-tooled it into Scout.com. This new site aggregated all kinds of information on high school and college team sports – with a heavy emphasis on recruitment. It was a godsend for professional scouts and college recruiters who, for the first time, could see and learn far more information about many more players on the Internet than they could ever discover the old-fashioned way, by making countless phone calls and travelling all over God's half-acre on personal visits. It was also extremely popular with avid football fans who used the site to see what players their favorite teams might be interested in. Fantasy leaguers and general fans loved it, too.

At one point we had 2.4 million unique visitors per month. The site was so popular that ESPN copied the idea with Scouts Inc. I figured our little start-up wasn't going to be able to hold out for very long against the marketing muscle of ESPN, so in 2005, I sold Scout Media, Inc. (the owner of Scout.com) to Fox Interactive Media, a unit of Rupert Murdoch's News Corp, for $68.5 million.

Along the way I was also involved in some real estate deals. After 9/11 a lot of people panicked, and property prices cratered. I didn't know much about real estate, but I figured land seemed too cheap to pass up.

Furthermore, if in fact the world was coming to an end, what difference would it make where my money was? So I bought land. My most lucrative deal was a few hundred-acre parcel in Florida that I bought for $5 million and later sold to the national home builder D.R. Horton for $42 million.

At one time in the early 2000's, I also became a partner in the Florida Panthers, the National Hockey League franchise in Miami. This came about, in part, because of my various connections in the South Florida business community. Wayne Huizenga, who had made his fortune in Waste Management, Blockbuster Video, and AutoNation, to name a few, had decided to sell his controlling interest in the Panthers, and associates of his who also knew me asked if I wanted in.

My answer was quick: "Hell yeah, I want in!" I love hockey! Love it. I was such a big fan that in the football off-season, when most players headed south for the warm weather, I headed north for the hockey. Montreal, Toronto, Vancouver – I loved them all.

I had become totally hooked on the game after making friends with Chris Chelios, at that time a defenseman for the Montreal Canadiens. Chris had spotted me in the crowd at a Canadiens game and banged the glass with his stick to acknowledge me, even though we'd never been introduced. We had dinner after that and became long-time friends. For the record Chris had one of the longest NHL careers ever (tied with Gordie Howe for most seasons), playing for the Canadiens, the Chicago Black Hawks, the Detroit Red Wings, and the Atlanta Thrashers, and he was inducted into the NHL Hall of Fame in 2013.

So when the opportunity to purchase an NHL team arose, I jumped in for a 6% piece. I figured that since I had given away so much money to friends and family, I deserved to spend some on something I enjoyed for a change. In those days NHL franchises were going for north of $100 million, but we got a deal from Huizenga, who was eager to back away from control.

When I look back, I marvel at how many great deals I was able to get into. Part of it, obviously, had little to do with my business acumen – I was an NFL celebrity who supposedly attracted instant attention to whatever venture I endorsed. And I had bucks to invest. Growth companies are always starved for cash, so I was an appealing prospect for a lot of companies, and as a result, I got to pick and choose the ones I thought were most promising. I'd like to think I made some substantive contributions to the marketing and management of each company. At a minimum I think I can claim to have had a good eye for exceptional talent and promising ideas.

One factor in my financial success, no doubt, was the intensity with which I jumped into the business world – especially after my retirement. I did so with an almost religious zealotry. In retrospect this made perfect sense considering my religious background. I always remembered the story in Matthew's gospel called the *Parable of the Talents* (a talent is a large monetary unit). In this parable a master, who is about to leave on a long journey, gives one servant five talents, another, two talents, and a third, one talent. While the master is away, the first two servants wisely invest their money and double it, while the third servant buries his talent. Once the master returns, the servants come to him to settle their accounts. When the master discovers what each has accomplished, he praises and rewards the two "good and faithful" servants who have been productive, and condemns the "slothful" one who has earned nothing.

This lesson stuck with me throughout my life: to be good and faithful is to be productive, and those who aren't, are "cast into the darkness." So, to some extent, my business success was always fueled by a fear of failure – and possible damnation. If I was to succeed, I needed to continue to make some sort of positive contribution – to society, and to my friends and family. If I failed to do so, God would be pissed off at me. I think, on some level, people seemed to sense this fear in me and often used it to their advantage. But I will discuss this much further in the next chapter.

If you were keeping score while I was rattling off all my business enterprises, you probably had me up to a few hundred million dollars. So what happened, you wonder? How did I go from a fortune like that to bankruptcy court? Well, that's an illuminating story. But before I give you the blow-by-blow, I have to provide some background on the family turmoil I was dealing with during this frenetic period of my life.

Top Left:
My First Communion picture at St. Mary's Byzantine Catholic Church in Youngstown. That day I received a cross which I ended up wearing in every game I ever played. It came out during games and was ripped off my neck numerous times, but it always found its way back to me. Sometimes I found it in my jersey pants, or stuck in my shoulder pads, or sometimes on the sidelines.

Top right:
My son Joe and I when I coached him during his soccer days.

Right:
At Super Bowl XXIX in Miami in 1995, I was involved in this staged promotional shot with a bunch of other guys. It is the first and only time my dad (right of me in this photo) and I ever actually touched a football together.

My daughters (from left to right) Sara, Rebecca, and Rachel in their annual dance recital picture — where they are wearing too much make-up applied by "Dance Moms," who seem to be living vicariously through their girls.

My daughter Rebecca and I swimming with the dolphins at Miami Seaquarium (owned by the great Arthur Hertz) on her birthday.

My high school quarterback coach, Jack Hay, is still a close friend. He was one of the first guys to really help me with my accuracy through the use of his net drill.

I am with Howard Schnellenberger (left) and Marc Trestman (right) on the sidelines immediately before I called the out route audible to Eddie Brown during the 50th Orange Bowl on January 1, 1984.

Icing down my ankle with Jim Kelly during the 4th quarter of a game already well in hand. I always thought it was an honor to be with Jim, who became my friend and mentor.

Earl Morrall, my first quarterback coach at the U, and I at a charity event on the west coast of Florida.

I had the honor of watching many Browns games with one of my personal heroes, Otto Graham.

Jimmy Johnson and I on the field for the pregame stretch before Super Bowl XXVIII in Atlanta, January 1994.

Jim Kelly and I reviewing plays before the 1988 Pro Bowl.

Throwing for the Hurricanes during my short-lived career at the U.

Jimmy Johnson and I leaving Tampa Stadium after a miraculous win over the Florida Gators in which I connected with Eddie Brown on a 12-yard touchdown with seven seconds left. 'Canes' love to beat the Gators.

The Browns QB "room" in training camp in the late 1980's (from left to right): Mike Pagel, Mike Norseth, me, Jeff Christensen, and Gary Danielson.

MOVE / Pass 6 texas split curl CB / FB stay
pass 6 TE deep ox flank?
36 power 27
★ 86 triple in
62 all curl (split) (look)
5 86 opt ser. left

I passes
pass 6 BAT, AI
pass 6 texas flank CB
★ MOVE PASS 9 1-6

SHOTS
MOVE red left wheel
left FLANK T.O.
flood rt opp flk rocket
Tess 18 lat to QB FLANK
red rt 96 split T.O.
red left 95 FLANK zoom
I 56 lat to QB pass
red rt opp 96 read HB50 split
E orbit pass 7 split TO ZIP
alert
TE HOTS 10 YD in

n Dw fly
QK sh lat
bone
m flank
Q/curl
Bunk
split zid flank Q
96 read
red rt
96 firm
un arr TO.

OPP. PASSES
MOVE ORBIT A
97 BAT
70 texas split curl / FB stay
Covey 96 firm HB arrow
move I rt orbit pass 7
B split T.O.
BI opp 80
92 special B.O.
split zoom pass 7 FB arrow
90 Backs left

3RD-3-6
86 split 6x
slot zoom 86, 66
TE M in 66
DBL DOG
fly 72 HB50
(Tem in) 86 TE cross Crack
Tem in flow 38 Backer
split zoom flow 39 Backer

10 YD in
Covey
more red rt orbit 96 firm HB arrow
red rt opp flk rocket 92 special B.O.
BI opp 80
BI rt opp split zoom pass 7 FB arrow
more red 62 QK sh lat
move YI rt zoom pass 6 FB arrow
WR switch rocket I rt Tess 38 chip
" " rocket red rt flow 38 BACKER
42 D. TO Z "I"

3RD DN Grn
fly 92
84 weakside go
flood zoom (fly) 92 smash TE B.O.

opp 44
opp 80
92 special or B.O.
42

ORANGE
14, 15 str. 17
16 George
66, 84, 86
66 slot cross
86 TE cross
62 all curl
fly 92
FLOOD FLY Dw
592 left
72 HB50
86 triple in
62 all curl

7-10
fly 92 flank hitch
66 go TE deep rex
86 go TE deep rex HB dart
fly 92, 86 zoom CB's
Tem in 86 firm out weakside
84 (weakside go)
Zoom (fly) 92 smash
66 slot cross

10+ fly 55n
fly 92 Bat flank z
86 BAT split lex
72 go zone SS I
fly 92 flank hitch
special ser. left

Grn zone lone
66 go TE deep rex
flood 72 go (HB dart) rt
fly 92 FLANK hitch
RUNS CRACK BA

INSIDE 10
84 weakside go
deep 40   92 s
flood zoom (fly) TE

MOVE
FLOOD rt
46, 40
66 slot c
86 TE C
MOVE YI MOTION
34 str.
90 zero

These are examples of the level of detail and specific plays and situations that I would run. On the other side of each of these was the official coaches' plans. When you see a star, especially multiple stars, those were plays I really loved given the personnel groupings on the field and the given situations (down and distance).

1st DN
m BI fly pass 6 (TEM)
n BI fly pass 6 texas split deep CB
PASS 6 FB arr.
n YI orbit Pass 6 texas slot BO.
J PB stay
M orbit I rt pass 7
I (BI) pass 7 FIANK PIN
m Dw fly 62, QK sh. BAT
TEM 86
Dw 62/63
92 texas, split CB
72 zone SSI
72 HBSO
opp 96 firm slot lex-0
m orbit 96 circle D-curl (BAT)
m BI fly 592
BI (Dw) holes 338 (318) (split T.O)
556

3RD 3-6
BATO
84, choice
scat 40 (fly 40)
d flank rex
86 split lex
86 DBL DoG (flank zie)
split zoom flow 39 cross
86 go DBL fin
86 go dart

3RD 10
86 go slot stem
86 zero CB
46 slot cross
flood left 73 go arr. HB
J FIANK CB
87 zone SSI (FB stay)

3RD 7-10
86 split lex
46 flank rex
86 zero CB's
86 (66) DBL DoG (zie)
Scat 40
84 (choice)
fly 92 (match)
split ind.
fly 92 BAT (Fl. zie)
split ind.
fly 72 HBSO (choice)
flood zoom 92 smash
86 DBL S.I weakside go slot stem

586 middle
SHOV. pass
DRG fly spec ser.
Flow 39 CK BACK

PIA as 1st DN
especially FIANK fin
Texas split CB
Tem 92
66 slot cross
Dw or Bare slot
556
592
BASE slot 86 TE cross
70 zone SSI (FB stay)
m Dw fly 86 triple in
opp 90 BACK left
86 DBL D CB

grn zone (10 yd)
opp 92 special
62 Aw
46 DBL D Q
62 FSI
46 flank Q
opp 96 firm HB arr
m Dw fly 40
pass 6 FB arr
m te I rt zoom
red 62 we hut (FAKE)
20 yd line
m Dw fly 62
592
72 HBSO
m orbit 96 fin
slot lex-0
B I left pass 6 ARR
46 flank Q
Dw 46 DBL D Q
deep 40
Dw fly 40
tem 92
RED rt opp 90 (BI) look left FIANK CB
I rt pass 6 texas FIANK CB

flood rt opp fk rock
toss 18 but te QB pass
m BI left fly pass 7
texas split T.O (1st DN)
I left pass 7 texas
split SI TO (2nd DN)
red left 71 zone split
SI T.O (2nd DN)
red left 97 split SI.T.O
(2nd DN)
flood left 73 go HB arr
Dw left 319 hide rt split

3RD
flood
84 (CB
scat 84 F
fly 92
62 FSI

3RD DN
flood 721
84 (slot c
zoom 92
scat 84
fly 92 (sm
DBL DoG
SCAT 84
Flood left
86 g

3RD
lex
fly
SCAT
sm

2
B

rocket red 96 read
HBSO 8 AV   46
wheel rt DOG ²⁰ʸᵈ CB ᶠᴸᴬᴺᴷ

62 (XF... ...)

RED GUN

| SHOTS | YI motion
46

90 All Curl look, 40

le   wheel rt flank T.O.
PASS8FIANK T.O. split CB deep

90 zero (CB)

red 90 zero T.O.
opp pass 7 split T.O.
red 96 split T.O.
opp 96(86) HBSO split zd
grn 46 D T·O
Int pass 6 or 7 teven split T.O.
91 bacher arrow

70 zone 55I In FB sly?

70 55I

tem 92,94 (alert HB late)

70(TS) D curl out Q
70 flank htch out Q

tem 92 bat HB over

ORANGE

DW

grn zone +10

86 TE cross
66 slot cross
46 J 7 in BOX
86 zero (CB X T.O.)
40, 66, 86

87 TE cross
67 slot cross
QK bat, 46

Squirm 96 QK, 46 split P
flank rex FB AV HB un
62 TE choice (ten
74 (alert hot) ten

MOVE orbit 96 HB arrow
deep 40, 62 deep m
move flank MOTiON

GRN +20 BASE

tem 92,94 alert HB late

MOVE zoom 62 FB arrow
62 FIANK rex FB AV HB unde
70 teven split Q HB unde
96 firm slot optn unde HB
MOVE 62 deep m flanker
87 choice (MOVE)
...... (HBS o

3RD DN 20 yd 6-9

Dhorel, 55 ser, Crush Bten
86, 86 split let
66, 66 flank rex
84 choice
fly 92 (HB delay out)
Split zoom 86(99) DQ fin o
.......grn TE sten (HB delay)
fly 92 smash TE BO. (out)

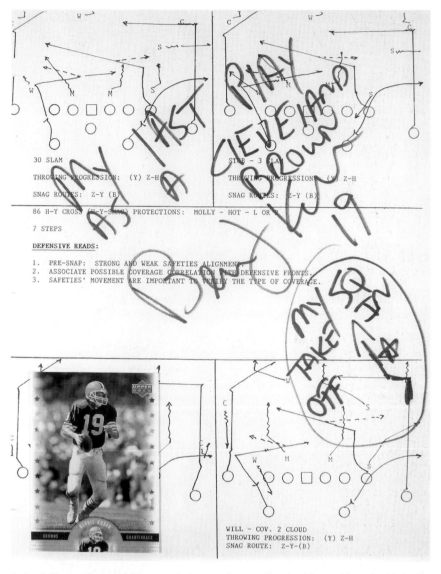

A play (with my adjustments) from my last game plan as a Cleveland Brown. Turned out to be the last touchdown I threw as a Cleveland Brown – a touchdown drawn up with Michael Jackson. The next day, the Browns released me.

We are backed up in our own endzone during the Jets double overtime game in 1986. In this photo, I am talking to Ozzie about a corner route which I threw to him about 25 seconds after this shot was taken.

My 1980's teammates on the Browns (left to right, top): Eric Metcalfe, me, Felix Wright, Kevin Mack; (bottom): Michael Dean Perry, Hanford Dixon (l) and Frank Minnifield (r), Webster Slaughter, Reggie Langhorne.

One of my favorite pictures – with Earnest Byner (left) and Kevin Mack (center). They were also one of my favorite backfield tandems.

Running the offense.

Gary Danielson, my main mentor, flashing me "The Rock." He's telling me not to give up, and that I can get them deep.

The first play in a two-minute drill in Cleveland Municipal Stadium against the Houston Oilers during Bill Belichick's first year as head coach. Matt Stover missed the game-winning field goal, an 18-yarder, by kicking it into the baseball dugout. I am pointing to the Mike linebacker who the line is supposed to block.

Under center during the Browns' heyday in the 1980's.

The great fans from the Dawg Pound traveled well, especially in the 1980's.

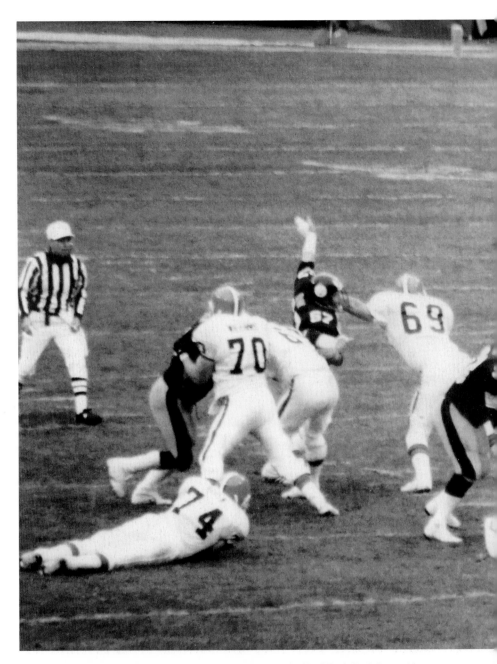

This play, a picture of which hangs in Kosar's Steak House at the Hard Rock Rocksino and in my living room at home, epitomizes the passion I brought to my career to get the right results. I am throwing over the Pittsburgh Steelers' Hardy Nickerson (#56 – a Super Bowl champ with the Buccaneers), but under Donnie Shell (#31 – another Super Bowl champ and Hall of Fame safety), with my 5'10" receiver Brian Brennan having to beat Rod Woodson (to the right of Brennan, yet

another Super Bowl champ and Hall of Famer). One of my best friends of all time, Paul Farren (#74), bottom left, has slipped and the defensive end is a millisecond away from breaking a few of my ribs. Out of respect and love for Paul, I take the picture down when I know he is coming over because I know he feels bad about it. But he saved me way more times than not – both on and off the field.

President Reagan visited us at practice at Baldwin-Wallace College in November 1988. By that time, I had the honor of being in his presence many times, so I was especially excited to have my teammates meet him.

George H.W. Bush on the campaign trail in the fall of 1988: (from left to right) Clay Matthews, Matt Bahr, Gary Danielson, George Voinovich, and me.

Signing autographs after practice at Browns training camp at Lakeland College. Back then, it was not uncommon to have 10,000 fans at daily practices. I tried diligently to sign every single thing someone put in front of my face, especially if it was from a kid.

Shaun Rogers (left), Drew Carey (center) and I at a Cavs game.

Hanging out with my friends at my long-running Bernie Kosar Charity Classic at Tanglewood in Bainbridge, Ohio: (from left to right) Mark Bryan, piano player for Hootie and the Blowfish; Bobby Monica, equipment manager for the Dolphins and the Browns; Jim Sonefeld, guitarist for Hootie; Darius Rucker, Hootie's lead singer and guitarist; and Top Dawg, Hanford Dixon.

Hanging out with Jason Krause (left), lead guitarist for Kid Rock and Kid Rock (right) at one of Chris Chelios' charity golf outings.

Spending time with Dennis Rodman at a Chris Chelios charity event.

All the "Dawgs" showing our support to Eddie Johnson at his charity event about three or four months before he passed away from cancer.

Enjoying some time with Chris Chelios (center) and Jeremy Roenick (right) at their charity event in Chicago.

At the Florida Panther purchase announcement in 2000, I was with the ownership team. From left to right: Alan Cohen, majority owner; Duane Sutter, head coach; Bill Torrey; and David Epstein.

I was with Carmen Policy (center) and Al Lerner (right) just after Commissioner Paul Tagliabue called to inform us that our Browns bid was accepted and the team would be returning to Cleveland for the 1999 season. Carmen and Al talked about how integral I would be to the team in the new era.

Chapter 9
DUTY

How about this for a disabled list? Let's start from the top down.

- Head: 15 concussions (officially), but more like 50
- Jaw and nose: over a half dozen breaks
- Teeth knocked out: lost count
- Shoulders: orthoscopic surgeries on both
- Ribs: a dozen broken
- Elbows: multiple surgeries on both
- Hip: bone removal for ankle surgery
- Left hand: gun shot (college)
- Fingers: all 10 broken multiple times
- Knees: both ACL's torn (anterior cruciate ligament)
- Ankles: both broken, multiple surgeries with pins and screws
- Toes: all 10 broken, multiple times
- Total surgeries: around 20
- Total broken bones: 50+ (not counting fingers and toes)

I think I've covered most of them. I do not rattle off this list to show you what a tough guy I am, nor to get your sympathy, nor to prove my commitment to winning football games. No, I rattle off this list to persuade you that I am something of an expert when it comes to pain.

Yet for all the physical pain I suffered in the game, none of it compares to the psychic pain I endured from my family and supposed friends. In fact it's more painful to talk about the mental scarring than the physical wounds. But I have to relate at least a glimpse of my family issues in order for you to have a better understanding of my financial problems. My relationships with family members partly explain some of the more bizarre things that happened to me throughout my lifetime. But they also illustrate a couple of other hard-learned lessons about growing up and about duty.

We'll begin with my dad, Bernie J. Kosar, Sr. I have already hinted at his difficult personality, but let me fill in the outline with a little more detail. My sister recognized his flaws much sooner than I did, and when she spoke to me about them, I refused to accept it at the time. I was in denial then, and unfortunately, remained so for a long, long time.

My dad grew up in Youngstown and graduated from Youngstown State University with a degree in industrial engineering. Like all of my family members before him, he worked for U.S. Steel while I was growing up. I always considered our family to be working class.

Then, when I was in high school, the plant shut down, and my dad lost his job. After a couple years he eventually got a sales job with a local generator company. Unfortunately, he wasn't very good at sales. He never mentioned earning any commissions, and I suspect he never did because I'm sure he would have bragged about it if he had. When he realized I was going to be drafted and play in the NFL, he quit his job to become my manager. That was the last regular job he would have, other than 'managing' my affairs (and cashing my checks), for a long time.

Even before all his unemployment problems, my dad took advantage of me. One time when I was a little kid, I spent days picking maybe five or six bushels of apples at a local park. I was going to sell these apples at the local farmers market for maybe $10 a bushel. Instead, the old man took them, and paid me 25¢ a bushel. He scammed his own kid for $50.

Around this same time, I had earned $2800 as a paperboy and intended to save all of it for college. That money disappeared, too. He even took possession of my coin collection, which I had started as a kid and had added to throughout my NFL career. God forbid I should ever ask to see it; when I once did, he blew up and indignantly claimed he was saving it for me for the future. I have yet to see these coins again.

These stories sum up a lot about what my dad thought about me, and for that matter, our whole family. We were his property – income-generating assets to be treated or mistreated however he saw fit. Publicly, he was not as openly callous and abusive to my brother and sister as he was to me. But behind their backs, he would insult my siblings liberally and use the C-word to describe my mother. This was a typical pattern for him: he would be gracious and complimentary to people's faces, but then viciously insult them to me behind their backs. It was all very upsetting at the time; but unfortunately, it was the only definition I had of 'normal.'

When I was in 5th and 6th grades, my dad didn't want me to play football. When he found out I was playing anyway, he beat me with his belt. He seemed to be opposed simply because he knew I loved it so much. This was another lifelong tendency which culminated years later when he torpedoed my opportunity to work in the Browns front office.

Despite all this, I always tried to please my dad, or at least pacify him. I think all kids try to please their parents. Kids want approval and are liable to feel guilty when they don't get it. Kids are too innocent even to consider the possibility that the problem might be their parent, not them. Add to that my conservative Byzantine Catholic upbringing (remember, I was an altar boy once upon a time). Then add the speech my father would lay on me constantly: "I am your father! Don't defy me! Do you see this gray hair? It means I am older than you. Which means I have more experience than you. Which means that I know more than you do. The Bible says you must honor your father..." That speech was a regular theme in my life, with a lot of variations, and usually spiced with obscenities I am leaving out. What was a kid supposed to do?

Then I went off to college for two and a half of the happiest years of my life. I was finally independent and, at least temporarily, free from the constant abuse and demands. I actually liked school and experienced my totally unexpected success in football. For once I was able to focus on my own interests and desires.

But I had to fast-track school and graduate early to resolve a bunch of problems. For one, I knew my family needed the money. Whenever I spoke to them, they would complain about their financial situation and express their belief that my professional success would solve all their problems. I also hoped this would be the case.

But the main problem was that I was afraid my dad was going to get both me and the U sanctioned by the NCAA. He was talking to agents left and right while I was still in school, which was a blatant violation. If he took money from them, we risked putting the whole program at Miami in jeopardy.[16] Knowing my dad's financial problems, I had to assume this was a distinct possibility.

After my college success, the Minnesota Vikings wanted me desperately. They traded two draft picks for the chance to pick me in the 1985 draft. Marc Trestman, who was my QB coach at Miami, had taken a job with the Vikings in the expectation that I would wind up there. I'm not sure if he has ever forgiven me for crossing up the Vikes. Actually, we remain good friends, and I am godfather to his kids.

In fact, I liked the Vikings, I loved Trestman, and I truly admired their head coach, Bud Grant. But I couldn't play in Minnesota. By that point, I had a serious girlfriend in Florida (Babette), and I figured that commuting between two states would be crazy enough; three states would be impossible. In addition my family laid a major guilt trip on me about being close to home and about my over-arching duty to them. I doubt they wanted me there for my own sake, but instead, so they could bask in – and take advantage of – my possible "celebrity." However, the deciding factor in my decision was my intense love for the Cleveland Browns, the one team I had always dreamed of playing for.

In those days you had to have graduated or used up your NCAA eligibility to qualify for the NFL draft. After only 2½ years in college, I still had plenty of eligibility left. But by taking the maximum number of classes year-round, I was very close to graduation. So when I realized I would wind up in Minnesota in the regular draft, I held off on one last course to avoid graduating before the April draft, knowing that I could wrap it up and graduate in time for the supplemental draft in late June or early July.

The supplemental draft was an oddity then, and still is today. It is designed to draft the occasional players who don't qualify in time for the regular draft, for any of a number of reasons, but who are available to play in the upcoming season. The League doesn't want to force them to sit out for an entire season until the next regular draft, for a variety of reasons. One is that the League worries (with some justification) that it will weaken its defense against accusations of monopoly power if it denies qualified players an opportunity to practice their profession. The League also worries that a player who sits out a year may not be in shape or may get into the kind of trouble that 21-year-olds from rough neighborhoods frequently get into when they have nothing better to do. I'm sure they also

---

16 I am often asked if I was aware of any 'pay for play' schemes at Miami like those most famously portrayed on the CNBC series *American Greed* involving Nevin Shapiro. The answer is no. All that nonsense took place well after I graduated.

worry about the revenue lost by not bringing a popular college star into the League ASAP. Popularity can be a diminishing asset.

So through my little gambit, I went into the supplemental draft. Ernie Accorsi, the Browns General Manager, was all over it. The Browns had traded a mess of picks to get Buffalo's number one choice so they could draft me. Art Modell even came to Miami in the middle of all this, supposedly to check out Eddie Brown, who was my best receiver in college and who went on to have a terrific 10-year career with the Bengals. But Gary Stevens, who was a coach at Miami, a great friend of mine and a native Clevelander, challenged Modell. "Gimme a fucking break," he told the Browns owner. "You ain't fucking here to see fucking Eddie. You're fucking here to see The Fucking Man!" Gary spoke in vivid Cleveland vernacular.

Everything clicked. The Browns drafted me in June of 1985. I was promised a $1 million signing bonus from the Browns, $360,000 of which was paid when I showed up for training camp. I thought all my problems were solved, and I was rich to boot. But when we broke camp, I found out, to my surprise, I was broke.

I discovered this when I attempted to buy a condo as my new Cleveland residence. After this failed attempt, my dad informed me that I had no money so I would have to wait for my first game check. For one of the first times in my life, I questioned him and continued to press him until he mumbled that my money had been spent on "expenses."

"What expenses?" I asked. "How much does it cost to drive from Youngstown to Cleveland?"

"I had to pay for agents," he replied.

The agents he referred to were guys he wanted to befriend – the local accountant, dentist, and attorney. I later learned that this was probably not where the money really went, because he paid some of these guys the *second* $360,000 installment of my bonus to buy out their 'agreements' after only a year later. So I can only assume that the first installment went to pay off a pile of debts he had accumulated during his unemployment. I was proud, though, to have discovered that some of it went to putting my brother through Baldwin Wallace College and my sister through Hiram College.

You might be wondering, "A dentist – as a sports agent?" Clearly, that choice had more to do with my dad wanting to play the role of local big shot than with any sound business rationale. But the dentist actually did me some good. He negotiated a five-year endorsement deal for me with

Converse at $150,000 a year, and I really liked the guy. I later suspected that that was the reason my dad bought him off (as well as the others). It seemed that if I got close to anyone, it threatened my dad's control of the situation, so that person had to go. At the time the dentist's son had recently committed suicide; but that didn't stop my dad from axing him, nor from laying the blame on me. The grieving dentist was told, "Bernie wants you to go," and that was that. The accountant also got pretty much the same treatment. That was a devastating sequence of events for me.

This kind of situation also regularly occurred on a personal level. For example, during my childhood, my cousin Johnny and I were best of friends, and I always admired him. When Babette and I were planning our wedding, his name was one of the first ones on our guest list. Naturally, we invited him to bring a guest as well. When my dad discovered this, he flipped out and complained about the expense, saying that if Johnny insisted on bringing a guest, he was not coming to the wedding. For once in my young life, at least temporarily, I stood up to him, and Johnny flew down to Miami with his girlfriend. However, without me knowing, my dad went to see Johnny before the wedding and told him that *Bernie* said he couldn't bring his girlfriend to the party. I haven't really spoken to Johnny since, and the event still makes me sick to my stomach.

This incident was just a preview of bigger things to come. Years later, Senior came with me to a meeting with Al Lerner, owner of the 'new' Browns. As a favor to Mr. Lerner, I had supported him, rather than the Dolan family (owners of the Cleveland Indians), in the City's choice for new ownership after Art Modell moved the 'old' Browns to Baltimore. The purpose of this meeting that my dad attended was twofold. We were supposed to discuss my possible role in future Browns operations, beyond the casual consultations and occasional appearances that I had been doing for the new regime. Second, we were supposed to discuss compensation for my new role, including a possible 5% stake in the ownership of the team. But almost at the outset of the meeting, my dad blew up at Lerner and yelled, "Fuck you! You use my son like a used condom!" He seemed to think he was going to intimidate Al Lerner, the owner of the Cleveland Browns, a multi-billionaire, and a former Marine. Needless to say, after a brief, stunned silence, the meeting ended abruptly, and I lost whatever chance I had to participate in the new organization. After that meeting I never had the opportunity to meet with Mr. Lerner again. My prospective

5% interest in the Browns wound up going to Carmen Policy, who became Browns President and CEO.

While this will surprise most people, the whole time I played pro football, I was never really aware of how much money I had. I never saw any actual bank statements or brokerage statements. Those went to my dad, who had power-of-attorney for all my affairs. I would only see statements he gave me based on who-knows-what kind of creative accounting. He would pay the payroll for some of 'our' companies with my personal earnings so that 'our' companies would appear profitable (I later found out). If I challenged anything, I would get the "I am your father" speech. When you're in the midst of an NFL season, it can be very difficult to be fully involved in every single financial decision. I also didn't have the time or the energy to do battle with the old man (whom, when I was younger, I naturally thought I could trust) while trying to get ready for the Steelers, for instance. So I let it slide.

At the time I was in my twenties. I told myself that I had a duty to give the old man a chance to succeed in business. I could afford it, and he needed some W's. I may have provided the most help of any son in the entire history of son-ship. But in the end, all my help amounted to what people in the rehab world call enabling.

My dad invested money like a gambling addict. He would buy 1,000 shares of some story stock (one whose publicity or *story* is more impressive than its actual value) at $25/share, believing somehow that a tip he picked up in Youngstown, Ohio, was unknown to Wall Street. When it dropped to $20, he would buy 2,000 more shares, figuring it had to be an even better bargain. Then he'd ride it all the way down. After this he would bet $100,000 on the next loser, to try to recoup his losses from the first loser. Then the stakes would go to $500,000 on the third loser, for the same reason. You get the picture.

A couple of sorry examples of my dad's investing style, on a business and personal level, were his insistence on buying an Arby's franchise in Virginia Beach, Virginia and starting a computerized greeting card company in the early to mid-90's. Now, Arby's started in Youngstown, my hometown, so you would think that Youngstown would be a more logical location than Virginia Beach. People knew me in Youngstown, and it would have been a whole lot easier to keep an eye on things. Cleveland, even, would have made sense. But no, it had to be Virginia Beach. From

Arby's perspective they probably couldn't sell the Virginia Beach territory to any other sucker. From my dad's point of view, it was an excuse to get away from Youngstown with his cronies and fool around. I protested, but I got the "I am your father" speech. As you might have guessed, our Arby's made no money.

Neither did the greeting card company. This fiasco – maybe better than any other – epitomized my father's lack of business sense and his shameless willingness to use me to take advantage of whatever influence I might have had among business people and celebrities. The product created by this company would allow consumers to create and print out sports-oriented greeting cards.

This was in the 90's, when e-cards were already well established, but my father was still sure this idea would be successful. To say the least, I had my doubts, but I agreed to get behind it. Despite all that had gone on in the past, I wanted to see him succeed in the hopes that giving him a win would provide some confidence and success that he could build upon. I did everything I could to get the thing off the ground. First I provided all the financing. Then I asked NFL stars like John Elway, Jim Kelly, Dan Marino, and others to become involved. I held press conferences, spoke to reporters, attended promotional events. I worked my ass off. But did my father appreciate it? Was the company profitable? Do I really have to answer either of these questions?

Despite all his failures, my father maintained a façade of the King Midas of investments. He set up a holding company called MF Investments. Guess what 'MF' stands for?

My brother Brian, unfortunately, was no better at investing than my dad. We got him a job out of college with a boutique Pittsburgh brokerage that handled a lot of deals for me. Then I helped him land a great position at McDonald & Co. in Cleveland. He then moved to a job at Sutro & Co. in San Francisco making $200,000 a year, but when the firm decided to move to L.A., Brian chose not to go. Instead, he wanted me to bankroll his own firm – with $10 million of my money – and provide deal flow.

I obliged, reluctantly. I knew I was throwing away my money, and I told my dad and brother, directly, that this company would fail, too. Nevertheless, being the good Catholic son, I gave my brother the $10 million to set up Cleveland Pacific Advisors, LLC.

Even this didn't satisfy my brother. He asked me to ask Al Lerner (the new Browns owner) to provide some investment capital, as well. That was one thing I wouldn't do; I could accept losing my own money, but not my friend's.

I did, however, discuss with Lerner my involvement in the company. He warned me that the company was bound to fail, and he advised me to back out. I told him I felt it was my duty to support my family and went so far as to tell him that my family loved me and appreciated what I was doing for them. I'll never forget his reply: "Bernie, you're even more gullible than I thought. Your family doesn't appreciate you – they're jealous of you. They want to be you." My Catholic brainwashing and guilt wouldn't allow me to accept Lerner's observations and advice. I wish he were still alive so I could admit to him that he was right and thank him for his honesty and concern.

Sure enough, in no time, Brian was back for more cash. So I put more multiple millions into a new vehicle, called Kosar Investments. But this time, I drew a line, sort of. I had a pretty good idea that my dad (unable to give up his investment addiction) was involved in Cleveland Pacific somehow, and that he would also be active in Kosar Investments. So I demanded that both he and my brother actually work this time instead of just moving money and pushing paper around. I also told him, "When you and Brian fail at this, don't come back to me for more. You can't come back and just say, 'I am your father.' That won't work anymore. You need to show me some respect."

Kosar Investments was a bust, of course, as I expected, but it turned out to be a turning point in my relationships with both Brian and my dad. Brian had invested in every dot-com fantasy he could find, from 1999 into 2000. I told him we were too heavily into tech, and the jackpot stories everybody was touting seemed too easy to me. His response: "You're stupid. You're a fucking dinosaur." I'm stupid? I'm the guy that financed his operation, twice, and paid private school tuition for his kids, but I'm stupid? Shortly after this exchange, the tech bubble burst, and the company blew up along with all the other dot-com disasters.

By now you are wondering, "Wait a minute... the Bernie Kosar of football fame was a dictator in the huddle. How does that Bernie let people walk all over him in private life? Football Bernie questioned authority figures on a regular basis. Football Bernie took command of some of the toughest guys on the planet. So why does he cave in every time his dad whips out the 'I am your father' speech? Why does he consent to a doomed investment scheme for his little brother, and then when it blows up, why does he double down on another one? How dumb are you, Bern?"

Believe me, I still ask myself these questions. And I'm still not sure I have a satisfactory answer. In the beginning, my focus was on football. I didn't need my dad marching into the locker room before a practice or a game to make a scene and get me to sign some papers (which he did). Better just to do what he wanted, try to make him happy, and get him out of my hair so I could try to win football games. I was willing to give him and everyone else in my family virtually anything in order to buy peace. Later, I was in scramble mode, involved in complicated business deals of my own. If I was going to be successful, I couldn't allow these kinds of family issues to become a distraction. At the same time, I was trying to keep my own, immediate family together. I had to reassure my wife who was accusing me of giving away all our money and claiming that I was planning on leaving her and the kids.

Plus, on the occasions when I did push back, my dad had deceitful countermoves. He would call important friends of mine, including, for example, our United States Senator, and moan, "Something's wrong with Bernie. I'm worried. He's not himself these days." He even went so far as to call Father Leo Armbrust (more about him later) – my close friend, whom he hated – in order to undermine me. This would trigger a flood of calls from concerned friends that I had to deal with, and which I could stop only by agreeing to whatever it was that the old man wanted.

Also – and I know this is difficult for people to understand – I told myself that tolerating all this abuse was my duty. It was my duty to take care of my family. It was my duty to share the wealth. It was my duty to help my dad and brother find some success. It was my duty to try to keep the peace. It was my duty to solve everyone else's problems. From boyhood I was raised to believe that all these duties were my primary responsibility. Nothing could be more important.

Maybe my career success led me to believe that with enough time and determination, I had a chance to solve any problem. I had won a national championship as a collegian. I had brought the Browns back from multiple touchdown deficits, repeatedly. I had marched them deep into the playoffs several times. Now it was my responsibility – my religious duty – to try to resolve my family's problems, even if I knew this was futile.

What I finally realized later in life was that duty has its limits. That's a tough lesson for a good little Catholic boy to absorb. The Ten Commandments say "Honor thy father and thy mother." Duty is a virtue, right? So how can virtue have limits?

Well, I've learned it does. You may feel it's your duty to jump into the rapids to save a person from drowning. But if in their panic they put a choke hold on you, and you both go down, well then, your sense of duty just got you killed.

My sense of duty was, at the very least, misplaced. I wasn't solving anyone's problems – including my own – by trying to buy peace. I wasn't being a good son, brother, or friend by enabling other people's harmful behavior. In attempting to make people more secure, I was, unknowingly, adding to their insecurity – and to my own. I wasn't making anyone happy, including myself, by religiously doing my duty.

Duties are not just random rules that someone made up in the misty past for no apparent reason. Duties are tied to some greater purpose. A soldier, for example, has a duty to obey orders from his superiors so that the entire unit can function together to serve a collective mission. But at the same time, the commanding officer has a duty to give legal orders. He can't just say, "Go execute those innocent women and children so that we can make a statement to our enemies." If he does, the soldier has a duty not to obey, the greater purpose being to end the war, not to make it worse. The same applies to football. You have a duty to 'just do your job' because other people are depending on you to do it, for their own survival and for the collective goal of winning the game.

In the game, however, it's crystal clear who your teammates are and who the opponent is. In my personal life, it was never so obvious. Your family and friends are supposed to be on your team. What are you supposed to do when instead of fighting *with* you they're constantly fighting *against* you? In the game I never had to worry about being tackled by one of my own guys. In my personal life, I had to worry all the time about being blind-sided by a friend or family member. Nevertheless, I remained dutiful, never really considering what greater purpose was being served. I just bumbled along doing what I thought I was supposed to.

Now I know that if things aren't working effectively, I need to stop and ask myself why I am continuing to do whatever it is that isn't working.

What greater good is being served? If I can't come up with anything, I no longer just zombie along because of some blind sense of duty. I know it's time to scramble and rethink the game plan.

By the way, in case you're wondering, my dad finally did get a steady job. He is the mayor of Canfield, Ohio. Yet to this day, he can't look me in the eye.

After all of this, I still love my dad, and I hope he is finally happy.

Chapter 10
HUMILITY

In football power is a pretty straightforward concept. It boils down to a combination of brute physical force and will power. The team that has the advantage in those two departments generally wins. Skill and strategy play a role, obviously. But if you can't control the line of scrimmage, offensively or defensively, you are in trouble. Your speedy receivers (or DB's) and your crafty game plan mean little if your linemen are routinely overpowered. It's as simple as that.

In personal relationships it's not always so straightforward. I am referring here to my failed marriage as a glaring example. Unpleasant as it is for me to recount, I share this saga with you for a few reasons. First, it is yet another true-life confirmation of the old saying that money doesn't buy happiness. Second, my marriage was, to some extent, a contributing factor to the financial downfall that I recount in the next chapter, although as you will see there, other more significant factors contributed as well. But the main reason I dredge up these memories is to make a point about an important lesson I learned, eventually, from the whole painful process: humility.

I met Babette, my wife-to-be, in college. In our first encounter she gave me the bum's rush. But after I quarterbacked the 'Canes to a National Championship, then all of a sudden I was Prince Charming. Maybe that should have been a clue, but I missed it at the time.

Unfortunately, I ran through a few other flashing amber lights as well. Shortly after we started going steady, she converted to Byzantine Catholicism (my religion) even though she was half Roman Catholic and half Jewish by birth. I should have been a little wary that someone who could flip her commitments to the Almighty that easily might not be all that serious about commitments in general. I should also have been more wary about her family history. Her own mom left her when Babette was only 13, which turned out to be a preview of things to come.

Unfortunately, that's par for the course for me. Women have never been my area of expertise, to say the least. In high school, and even at Miami before Babette, I was awkward and nervous around girls. I was always worried that I would make a fool of myself. They had to approach me. I never approached them. So when Babette did that, boom, I was in love. She was the first and only girlfriend I had in college, and it stayed that way till we got married in 1990.

You're probably thinking that eight years is a long time to go steady. But I had a pro football career to pursue, which was an all-consuming passion; so I put family formation on the back burner. Then one day, I heard the biological clock ticking. I know that is generally thought to be a female phenomenon. But in my case, it dawned on me that if I didn't take action, I could be a 60-year-old father with an NFL-beaten body, trying to play catch with an eight-year-old kid. I didn't want that, so I proposed. Looking back on it, I realize I probably should have factored far more considerations into the decision.

Once we were married, the trouble started immediately. By 'immediately' I mean in the limo from the wedding ceremony to the reception. Out of nowhere she started harping at me about how we weren't going to spend the whole evening with my friends, about how I had to be nice to her family (like I didn't know that), yada yada yada.

You would also think that after eight years of courtship I would know someone better than I knew Babette. Call me clueless. Put it down to a long-distance relationship that kept us apart a lot. Both legitimate issues. But a big problem revolved around personality issues.

I think it can be argued that we all have ranges of personality disorders – from quirks and neuroses to more serious mental conditions. However, I think that sometimes we are too quick to put labels on these conditions and then immediately assume the worst about them. Instead, I feel people should try to accept them and see them as possible gifts rather than liabilities. I realize this is far easier said than done, and to do so requires candid honesty, both with yourself and with others. I think I've finally come to develop this kind of honesty, and the process has been very enlightening. It has also helped me form more satisfying relationships and lead a happier life.

I wasn't always able to look at things this way; especially after I discovered Babette might have BPD (borderline personality disorder). In the midst of our marital problems, in order to appease Babette, I had agreed to visit a therapist (whom *she* had chosen) because she was convinced that I was the problem. In our meetings the therapist suggested that I was probably married to a person with BPD, so I invited him to stay at our house for a week to observe our situation and possibly verify his diagnosis. After only two days he confirmed that not only did Babette have BPD, but her mother did as well. He said he literally feared for me.

In the 90's most people were unaware that BPD even existed, but there is a significant bibliography on it now. If you're interested, check out any number of books with 'Walking on Eggshells' in the title. This phrase perfectly captures the nature of the disorder since anyone who interacts with a person who has BPD feels like he or she is constantly walking on eggshells.

According to these texts, people with BPD believe that nothing is ever their fault. It's always your fault. There is nothing you can do to please them. I tried to buy peace with Babette, like I did with my dad and brother. I provided her with whatever she wanted. I bought houses for her and for her relatives. I gave her money to invest (and to her mom, as well, who miraculously reappeared a few months before Babette married me – another clue I missed). More important, beyond these material gifts, I devoted considerable time and focused attention to her and to what she deemed was important. But nothing ever seemed to satisfy her.

While I was playing, my obsessive concentration on football probably didn't help the situation. I was on the road a lot, and even when I was home, I spent a lot of time watching game film and doing my football homework. Despite this, I was always attentive to her needs – but because these needs were constantly changing, I was always walking on eggshells. After I retired from football at the end of the 1996 season, the situation went from bad to worse.

I could give you a thousand specific situations of walking on eggshells, but I will spare you the grief and relate just one. In the middle of the Wild Card deal that I mentioned in Chapter 8, I passed out debit cards to my kids. I was being the benevolent dad but also conducting some personal market research on the utility of the debit card concept. Babette went nuts. She insisted the kids were way too young for that kind of financial responsibility, and she complained that I was spoiling them. Six months later, after the debit cards were used up, the kids came back to me – this time asking for credit cards. Taking into consideration Babette's previous reaction, I said no and told them they were too young. Nevertheless, she flipped out again. "You're going to let your girls wander around town with no money? What if they get into some kind of trouble, what are they supposed to do? It's not safe!" I couldn't win.

By the time our oldest girls hit their teens, Babette started going out and doing the things she said she always wanted to do. By then, since I was out of the game, I was staying at home more to take care of the kids, which she had said she wanted me to do – and which I actually loved. However, it seemed my presence threatened her importance with the kids, at least in her mind. It was as if she were angered by my ability to handle all the family responsibilities on my own. So she did her best to drive me out.

People can be very inventive, and the human brain has a remarkable ability to create its own reality. Babette created the following one. She would scream and yell, loud enough for the kids to hear, that I was beating her. She would call 911. Nothing ever came of it because when she would go ballistic on me, I would go out of my way to avoid conflict or even the appearance of retaliation. I would stick my hands in my back pockets and try to absorb whatever abuse came my way.

Eventually, I had to leave. I knew it wouldn't put an end to the insanity, but I hoped it would at least reduce the torture for our kids of having to listen to their parents fighting all the time.

Even after I moved out, I still spent a fair amount of time with the kids. When I would discover that Babette was off on one of her long weekends and had arranged to outsource the kids somewhere, I would fly back down to Florida to take care of them. I didn't want them to be 'backpack kids,' getting randomly shunted off on friends and family. I owned a Lear jet at the time, which somewhat simplified the logistics of all this shuttle parenting. At the same time, however, I was trying to do deals with the likes of InterActiveCorp and Fox News Corp. while also involved in bringing the Browns back to Cleveland. So I was bouncing around from Cleveland to New York to Florida, or the reverse, on a daily basis at times. It was a crazy situation.

We did the separation/reconciliation thing a few times before we finally got divorced in 2007. Ultimately I came to the realization that my kids were suffering from these intolerable circumstances. That's when it finally sank into my concussed brain that I was in a hopeless situation.

You might logically wonder why anyone would tolerate such misery for that long. Well, one obvious reason was the kids. I still hoped we could create that ideal, storybook family. Religion factored into it as well. In Byzantine Catholicism, and for that matter in Catholicism in general, marriage is a holy sacrament. You swear an oath before God. I take such oaths seriously.

What I came to learn was that power, in the football sense, is irrelevant in personal relationships. For one thing, brute physical force is off the table entirely. But even will power was useless in my marital travails. I finally had to face the fact that I couldn't solve everyone's problems. No amount of money was going to buy peace and happiness. No amount of effort or forgiveness was going to change anybody's personality – or personality disorder. So my determination gave way to extreme self-doubt.

Powerlessness is a hard lesson for a determined person to accept. In the game, I never quit. Even if I was losing, even if I was hurt, quitting was not an option. I am proud of the fact that in 12 pro seasons, I was never wheeled off the field. You suck it up, you try harder; but you don't quit.

Unfortunately, however, that mindset didn't help me at all in my personal affairs, and it may actually have been an obstacle. Ultimately, I had to face the fact that being good at one thing, like football, for example, doesn't necessarily mean you're good at everything.

It's odd – if anyone had ever told me I should take up singing, I could have easily replied, "Uh, I'm not qualified. Not even a little bit." I've had the opportunity to sing *Working for a Living* live on-stage with Prince and Huey Lewis, and *Mustang Sally* with Hootie and the Blowfish, and *Take Me Out to the Ballgame* with Kid Rock. For all three I 'Milli Vanilli'ed' my way through, so the whole world knows I can't carry a tune in a wheelbarrow. But when it came to dealing with my marriage, it took a long time – maybe too long – to realize I just wasn't qualified to handle the situation I was in. Not even a little bit.

That was hard. Admitting fallibility was more painful than all the injuries I ever racked up in football, combined. But the moment that you admit you are not Superman, you have discovered a new virtue: humility.

Chapter 11
MONEY: PART II - THE FALL

Cute, huh? I use Chapter 11 to tell you the story of my bankruptcy. Hopefully you'll appreciate my clever use of numbers.

Now that you have plowed through the last two chapters and have some idea of the 'help' I had from my family in 'managing' my money, we can dive into where some of it went, to the best of my knowledge, belief, and recollection. While I did require my dad and brother to promise me they would save all financial records, whenever I asked to see them, the documents seemed to have mysteriously disappeared. Occasionally, they would reappear when, and only when, it was convenient and beneficial for either of them.

My first significant deal, as you may recall, was the Quarterback Club, which I started when I was still playing. But as well as it worked out for the other members (and, I would argue, for all players), it eventually wound up costing me a bundle.

I need to explain that QBC didn't just do licensing deals. While I was involved, we invested some of the licensing money in other business deals. For example, in 2001, we invested in FieldTurf, a new form of artificial playing surface. I single out this investment because we viewed it not only as a money-maker, but also as a life-saver. We had all played on AstroTurf, which up to that point was touted as the answer to the sloppy playing conditions of natural grass in rainy or snowy weather in places like Cleveland, Ohio. AstroTurf allowed for faster play and sharper cuts, all right, but it also ushered in a whole new spectrum of injuries (remember 'turf toe'?). Everybody joked that it was like playing on fuzzy concrete. But if you got slammed to the ground on that stuff, it was no joke. So we jumped on FieldTurf, literally.[17]

---

17 Eventually, we sold our interest in FieldTurf to a hedge fund, and all the guys shared in the joy. This product made the news more recently. Evidently, for the Pro Football Hall of Fame game in 2016, someone used the wrong paint for the logos and hash marks, which ruined the playing surface and caused the cancellation of the game.

At one point I managed a lot of these investments myself. But my father and my brother begged me – *begged* me – to let them handle the investments. This took place while the whole Cleveland Pacific/Kosar Investments fiasco was occurring – along with my marital difficulties. I had so many other things going on that I relented, figuring I could keep an eye on things and prevent any serious disasters. Wrong.

I set up a meeting for my dad and brother to present themselves to members of the QBC and various owners and League officials. The two of them got so excited at the idea of meeting all these dignitaries that the night before our meeting, they went out to a strip club and got totally wasted. I didn't find out until the credit card bills arrived that they had been rolled for over a $100,000 in charges that they had hidden from me. I know that sounds impossible; but evidently, they were too blotto to resist signing the stream of charges that the strip club management was busily inventing backstage.

At the time I wasn't aware of this little fiesta. The following morning, all I knew was that I was in a conference room full of NFL big shots, and my father and brother were AWOL. I tap danced for a good half hour before the two of them staggered in, and I mean staggered. They were still so hung over that it was pretty obvious what had happened. Either they had both come down with the Ebola virus, or they had drunk themselves half to death. They tried to speak, but they were sloppy and incoherent. So now *my* cred was in serious jeopardy for having invited these two. In desperation I came to the rescue and made their pitch for them.

That worked, at least as far as getting the OK for my father and brother to do the investing. But they managed to blow through all the money at their disposal – in a wide range of dumb investments – even faster than I could imagine. They blew it all. To make amends, I forked over to QBC a big chunk of my profits from other investments.

Another investment, in Envision Pharmaceuticals, whose founder is an amazing businessman and friend, should have been a big payday, too. Envision was the benefits management company that sold to a private equity firm for around $1 billion, and in which I had an initial 10% stake. Unfortunately, my stake was not in the form of publicly traded stock that I could sell freely. This was a closely held, private firm, and it's hard to know what those are worth until somebody actually buys them. Furthermore, my stake was contingent on a few factors. One contingency I agreed to was that my family members could not interfere in the business, and if they did, I would return my holdings. As you might have guessed, I couldn't prevent my family from meddling, so I was obliged to give back much of my holdings. The principal owner ultimately bought out what was left of my stake for $160,000 in my bankruptcy, in 2009, four years before Envision matured and hit the jackpot in the private equity sale.

As I indicated earlier, my best real estate deal was the D.R. Horton transaction, in which I sold a $5 million tract in Florida to the home building company for a theoretical $42 million. I say theoretical because we received only $17 million up front since my brother, instead of accepting an immediate $38 million, negotiated a three-part deal. The back end payments never materialized because the housing crisis of 2008 intervened, and Florida land values collapsed.

Despite these setbacks, and a pile of taxes I paid on the deals that did work out, I figure that at my high point, I might have been worth maybe $75 million. That's not the nine digit net worth it might have been without the setbacks, but still, by any sane standard, it's a ton of money. So what happened, you wonder?

I confess that I spent pretty liberally at the end of my 'rich' period. The good news is that I didn't blow it on drugs or gambling or the kinds of vices to which many other rich guys have fallen victim. But the bad news is that I still had a burn rate (should I say 'Bern rate'?) of maybe $4 million a year. I had multiple homes, plus I bought houses for a number of family members. I had my own Lear jet, which cost ten grand per trip, times 50 trips a year. I paid private school tuitions for a lot of kids in the family, besides just my own. Nobody wanted for anything when the Bank of Bernie was in business. And the bank paid out generously for a long time.

I was also able to sock away a significant amount of trust money for my kids. I'm not sure how much of this is still around because I found out that my dad would use the power-of-attorney I had given him to 'invest' the kids' trust money in some of his cockamamie story stocks. So I set up separate trusts that he didn't know about for each of the kids. In any event, once you put money into trusts, it's not yours anymore.

The divorce settlement with Babette was also expensive. She used multiple attorneys (the number approached double digits) who were all paid by me. The settlement boiled down to $3 million, plus child support of $15,000 a month.

I also wrote out seven-digit checks to a number of causes that I supported. I mentioned the business school at Miami. I also helped with Haitian earthquake relief. I set up a 501(c)(3) to support scholarships and youth camps and sports facilities for inner-city kids. These only scratched the surface of the number of charities I supported with both my time and financial contributions. I could be accused of giving away more than I could afford to, but I viewed it as a way to make sure that at least *some* of my money would be put to good use.

The fact is, I had a sense all along that my father and my brother were burning through the money generally faster than I could make it. Recall that the original money grab for Cleveland Pacific was $10 million, and that I doubled down before I drew the line with those two, and that I then discovered they had racked up another $5 million or so in expenses that I had to cover. That fiasco, along with the Virginia Beach Arby's debacle and various other smaller losers too numerous to recount, basically meant that they were blowing through it as fast as I could make it – sometimes faster. As a practical matter, I was functionally bankrupt three or four times before I finally had to file in 2009. I came to view the 'make a pile, lose a pile, make another pile' routine in football terms. Sure, you get sacked sometimes, but you don't quit. You get back in the huddle, and you go for another scoring drive.

The ultimate sack, however, came in 2008, when the real estate market went to hell. I mentioned how that debacle had cut my D.R. Horton deal practically in half. What I didn't know was that my dad and brother were borrowing on the $10-20 million that was supposed to come in from Horton (but never did), and then they couldn't meet the debt service of a few hundred thousand dollars per month – for which I became responsible. By that point, I owed various banks north of $20 million. I had no spare collateral lying around to give them. And the debt service, plus the taxes and other carrying costs of my mini-empire, not to mention the personal spending levels to which I had become accustomed, turned out to be more than I could handle. So in June of 2009, I filed for Chapter 11. Seven months later, it was converted to a Chapter 7 bankruptcy, meaning there was no hope.

I know all this is difficult, maybe even impossible, for a person with an average income to comprehend. I know you are still wondering after all my testimony, how I could lose everything. "Bernie," you are thinking, "we know about the real estate collapse. And we understand charitable giving and trusts for the kids. And we even get the family issues, sort of. But still... *everything?*"

OK, there are some psychological factors that come into play on top of all the facts I have already given you. The first one applies not just to me, and not just to jocks. You see it happen with other celebrities and with lottery winners and with people who inherit fortunes. I have even seen it with other business people who seemed to be sophisticated and money-smart, and then – boom!

For most people, money is a necessity. You gotta pay the rent and buy the groceries, etc. And if your life depends on something, you guard it carefully and you don't waste it.

Now, many people may not live on the brink of desperation. Many people make more than the minimum and live in nicer homes, take vacations, put kids through college, and have a decent retirement. But those folks have to watch it, too. Typically, they are not socking away big money. They may be ahead of the game, but not by much. A lost job or a serious illness could wipe out whatever they have. So they always think of money as a necessity, even though they may have a little more than they need. They watch the budget and try to handle their resources with some care.

Then there is the tiny minority that is just swimming in money, like I was. At some point you have so much money you stop worrying about it, especially when big waves of it keep coming in and the flow seems infinite. At that point you have so much income that you don't think about outflow anymore. You just float on the excess.

And even when the tide ebbs and that ocean of money drains down to a few inches and your ass is now touching the sea floor, you still don't worry about it because you just know that another big pay day is on its way. When it has been so easy to generate money in huge quantities, why worry? You'll recover. You'll be able to take care of it all.

What I didn't realize is that you can't count on the flow to last forever, just like an NFL quarterback cannot rely on his ability to elude defenders and complete passes forever. To the extent that my celebrity was a factor in opening doors that are closed to most people, fame can turn out to be a fading asset. And when you do hit bottom, and you have no capital to put into new deals, your appeal as a potential business partner also fades away. But I wouldn't quit because I knew I could bounce back like I always had and keep playing, even if hobbled.

But the business world didn't view my bankruptcy as an off day. It was more like a career-threatening injury. You hear stories about venture capitalists who won't touch start-up entrepreneurs *unless* they have been through bankruptcy, like it's a baptism by fire. That may be true for the young bucks. But when you're pushing 50, if you hit bottom, you may not be able to shake it off and come back next week to atone. Yet you don't quit; you scramble back to square one and start over.

The other psychological factor is more personal to me. I knew my dad and brother were blowing through money like hell won't have it. I knew that the powers of attorney I had given them were being used and abused. I knew I was doomed eventually; it was just a matter of time. But believe it or not, I firmly believe I did the right thing.

Obviously, if you're counting how many zeroes trail my current net worth, I was an idiot. But I realize – especially now – that my greater goal was peace. At first my goal was family peace. I attempted to purchase this peace with an admittedly careless generosity. Clearly, that didn't work. And unfortunately, by the time I figured that out, it was too late from a financial point of view.

But, ultimately, I did purchase peace *for myself.* My conscience is clear. I gave all the support I could to my family, as well as to many others. I am free from any remorse about not doing enough. I left it all on the field, so to speak. Sure, I wish I had a few mil left in the bank, but not at the expense of a lifetime of self-recrimination.

A very successful friend of mine recently told me that the second-hardest thing in business is making a lot of money. The first-hardest thing, he continued, is hanging on to it after you made it. Well, I'm living proof of that theory. But even if I'd met this guy a long time ago, I'm not sure it would have made any difference

Chapter 12
CHARITY

From an early age there was always a dynamic tension in my life between what I wanted to do and what I was supposed to do. What I wanted to do, as you know, was play football, to the point of becoming that obsessive-compulsive monomaniac that I described earlier. What I was supposed to do, I firmly believed, was attend to the demands of my family. Those two goals, as I have described at length, were often in conflict.

In my earlier years I juggled 'want to' and 'supposed to' as best I could. You might fairly claim that I achieved more success with 'want to' (my football career) than I did with 'supposed to' (my family's happiness). But that conclusion would not make my story unique in any way, or even unusual, for that matter. I suspect that many people have had more success at what they wanted to do than at what they were supposed to do. It goes back to that 'discretionary effort' thing I discussed earlier.

To me, a more interesting question is what happens when something you want to do comes into conflict with another 'want to.' This is a question that didn't hit me until later in life, after I was out of the game. To explain this dilemma, I have to rely on a quote from Abraham Lincoln:

"With malice toward none, with charity for all..." [18]

Today, we typically use the word charity to describe donations of money, or volunteer effort, to the poor or to worthy causes. But in Mr. Lincoln's time, the word had a broader meaning: namely, acts of kindness and generosity directed to other people in general, not just to those in need. The word charity actually comes from the Latin word *caritas*, which means caring. Charity, in this sense, came into my life in 1990, which was

---

18 These famous words, as you might know, come from Lincoln's Second Inaugural Address. They were his eloquent attempt to start patching things up near the end of the Civil War.

the year I got married and started a family. I had always given money to charities in the past, but it wasn't until I had kids of my own that I began to understand charity in the classical sense that Mr. Lincoln meant.

Until 1990 my football career had been downright blessed from the very beginning. In 1983 at Miami, the Hurricanes won the National Championship. The following year, we went to the Fiesta Bowl. In 1985 I gained a starting role with the Browns. We then proceeded to go to the playoffs in each of the next five years. I think the only other quarterbacks to do that in their first five seasons were Dan Marino and Joe Flacco.

I mention this not to brag about my glory years, but to describe the high point from which my professional career began to decline. In 1990 I threw a career-high 15 interceptions, and the Browns went 3-13. Ugh. The next year (1991) wasn't much better (6-10). In these years the Browns' chronic problems with draft picks were beginning to catch up with them. On top of that, I had issues of my own. I was out most of 1992 with a broken ankle. I was cut in the middle of the '93 season, as noted earlier (I have to concede that when Coach Belichick cited my "diminished skills," he wasn't just reacting to my rebellious play-calling).

The point is that the downfall began right around the time I got married and started having kids. Now, I'm not saying that my family killed my career. Far from it. At the time it didn't even occur to me. The fact is that after nine seasons in the League, I had broken a lot of bones and undergone a lot of surgeries. I was a very old 30. There is no question that my physical skills had diminished, at least somewhat.

But in later years, I began to wonder if the growth of my family and the decline of my career were pure coincidence, or if one had something to do with the other. The truth is that once I had a family, my focus shifted. Football was no longer the center of my life. I had these beautiful little babies that I adored. They were the center of my life now. I had so much fun with them. I dragged mattresses into the living room so that we could wrestle and bounce around. To this day I love bombing around my farm on ATV's with the kids, or when the weather is nice, just lounging around the pool together.

For the record I don't mean to suggest that I skipped practices to go home and take care of my kids when they were little, because I didn't. Having kids did not make those kinds of demands on my time. It was more of a mental thing. My primary concern became the welfare of my babies. And my concern didn't flow so much from 'supposed to,' the way it had with my parents and siblings, as it did from 'want to' – from some inexplicable urge to make my children happy, healthy, and strong. I cared for them, for their own sakes, and they gave me more joy than anything else I had ever experienced before. Thanks to them, I had unwittingly discovered a new blessing in life: namely, charity, in the old school sense that Lincoln intended.

This transformation, however, eventually made me wonder about a question I had never considered before: is charity incompatible with other, more personal goals? Let's suppose, for example, that I had come into the League with a couple of kids to whom I was totally devoted. Would I have had that obsessive-compulsive sense of dedication to the game that I believe is so critical to success? Would I have made the playoffs in my rookie year? Would I have had that successful run in the late 80's? And if I had, would I have been as concerned about my kids as I am now, or would they just have been part of the background noise in my life that I tried so hard to block out in those days in order to focus on winning? In other words is it possible to reach the pinnacle of your profession without being fanatical about it? And if it isn't, does that mean you have to abandon charity while you pursue your own personal goals?

In the old days men typically didn't worry about these questions. The arrangements were pretty cut and dried. Dad went to work, and his job was to rise through the ranks as high as possible to provide as much financial support as possible for his family. Mom's job was to stay at home and raise the kids. Dads certainly cared for their children on some level, but their primary responsibility was to provide financial security, essentially by successfully achieving their own particular career goals. As for whatever Moms may have wanted to achieve for themselves – well, most men just didn't consider that back in the day, and regardless, the women generally kept that to themselves and took care of the family.

Nowadays, however, work-life balance is a huge concern. Women (deservedly) are everywhere in the workforce, juggling career and kids. More and more men are pitching in on the child-care front, some voluntarily, some not so much. Either way, it's getting harder and harder for people to devote themselves totally to career achievement in the way I did. If you're doing well enough financially, I suppose you can hire a nanny (and Babette had two – which I hated), but where is the charity in delegating the care of your own children to other people?

I'm not saying everybody has to make a choice between being obsessive-compulsive or being Mother Teresa. Obviously, most people fall somewhere in between those extremes, and many of them achieve significant personal success even with a 'family first' commitment.

But I wouldn't call it work-life balance: I would call it work-life compromise. If you want to go for the gold and become the CEO of a major corporation, or a U.S. Senator, or whatever the highest level of your own chosen profession may be, I think you have to be totally focused on that – stubbornly, obsessively, compulsively. At least I had to be. If you want to get to that level, nothing can distract you.

If that's your dream, I can understand completely. I went for it in my field, and I had the kinds of thrills that very few people get to experience. I loved it so much that I would give up just about anything to go back to the glory days of the late 80's and see if my Brownies and I could win a ring.

On the other hand the 'just about anything' I would give up does not include my children. I wouldn't give them up for anything. This may well mean that I couldn't win that ring of my fantasy even if God transported me back to 1985, because my kids are now my primary concern in life. I'm not trying to dictate which road a person should take. That's his or her call. I am saying two things. First of all, it is a choice, and it's a tough one. I don't believe you can have your cake and eat it, too. I know people who think they can have it all, but I just don't buy it. I think they're setting themselves up for disappointment if they expect to be one hundred percent happy, one hundred percent of the time. If you want to fulfill your maximum personal potential, you can't be bothered with anything else. Charity is a distraction you cannot afford. You can't let the soccer game or the dance recital or the quality time interfere with the conference call or the business trip.

Second, and more important, individuals need to think long and hard about this choice, particularly young people. They need to be honest with themselves about all possible consequences. Is your personal goal so important that you would spend your whole life concerned only with yourself and not others? On the flip side, if you don't chase your dream, will you resent your loved ones for holding you back? It's a tough decision that requires serious thought. What I am sure of is that you don't want to turn 50 and then start contemplating the shoulda-coulda-woulda's of your youth, if only you had been paying attention at the time.

Chapter 13
CONFIDENCE

The spotlight of public attention makes people do strange things. We've all seen what happens when the fan-cam throws somebody's image up on the Jumbotron. They go bonkers. They jump up and down, wave their arms wildly, make funny faces, do finger horns behind their friend's head, and all kinds of crazy stuff they would never in a million years do if they were just walking down the street. The camera can turn normal people into goofy circus clowns.

I suppose this is because public attention is so rare for most people that it seems precious. Most people never get the 15 minutes of fame that Andy Warhol talked about, so if they get even five seconds, some get so excited that they lose control. And everybody in the stadium who's watching gets a huge kick out of it, partly because they know full well that they'd do the exact same thing if only the camera would give *them* five seconds.

I have always had the opposite problem. I have spent my whole adult life in the public eye and not always in a flattering light. I have had national TV cameras focused on me since I was a teenager at the University of Miami. And when you're in the NFL, publicity just follows you around like a shadow, especially if you are a quarterback, and especially if you play on successful teams, which I did. And even after you are out of the game, if anything goes wrong in later life, as it certainly did in mine at times, the floodlights of public attention flash back on, and your problems become national news. The media and its consumers seem to love 'trouble in paradise' stories.

I'm not complaining about the pub. I understood from college on that publicity was part of my job. And when you spend your formative years constantly in the limelight, public attention becomes a norm you get used to, even if it is not always pleasant. No, my message here is this: if you crave fame, you may not be prepared for what might be in store for you.

To be blunt, I am not naturally a gregarious guy. I love hanging out with my kids or a group of buds, but crowds of strangers actually make me nervous and uncomfortable. I try to be as friendly as possible, but it takes an effort. I'm sure I would have been a lousy politician.

Despite my chronic case of nerves, I do find it fun to interact with fans during personal appearances. Most folks are really thrilled to talk to a celebrity – since talking to a celebrity is as close as they may ever come to being one themselves – and you can just tell how happy they are to have the opportunity. We chat, we do the selfies, I let them play with my Super Bowl ring, I sign autographs, and hopefully they get a kick out of it.

I'm still blown away by the stuff people want me to sign: Browns hats and jerseys and memorabilia, naturally. But I've also been asked to sign a lot of body parts – a total too numerous to recount. A female fan once asked me to autograph an image of me that was tattooed just slightly north of her pubic region (I declined that one). Some people show up with life-size posters of me in my playing days and lug these monsters around a public venue. One guy at an Akron Racers event had two bobbleheads of me, one as a Miami Hurricane from thirty-some years before, and one as a Cleveland Gladiator. Incredible. So whatever uneasiness I feel in crowds is balanced out to some degree by the gratification of knowing I made somebody's day.

But then there are fans who go overboard. Inevitably, in a line of 50 people waiting patiently for an autograph, there is one guy who needs to tell me his life story, or his theories on Browns ownership, or his views on world affairs. Dude, there are 50 people waiting behind you. Forget about my time. What gives you the right to eat up *their* time? Are you even aware of them? Not likely. Instead he is hypnotized by his moment of celebrity and oblivious to everything else.

I once had a guy bust in on a conversation I was having with George W. Bush at a Hall of Fame event. Don't ask me how he managed to blast past the Secret Service detail, or how he managed not to notice he was interrupting a former President. This dude was in his own zone. Two times I have had guys recognize me in the men's room and turn to face me while still peeing. Both times I was left with pee splatter on my pants, which was very difficult to explain to others.

I have also had people swoon over me – and I mean literally. I'm not bragging here, because I know it's not actually about me and my own personal magnetism. They don't even know me, and I'm certainly no cutie anymore. It's probably an emotional reaction to being in the presence of somebody famous, and any number of famous people would get the same reaction. But when it happens, you have to be prepared for the possibility that this person might actually faint on you and collapse to the ground. And if you're thinking that catching fainting beauties and saving them from a nasty fall sounds appealing, let me tell you, it can be scary. When someone starts to wobble, I immediately think: I'm not 23 anymore; my reaction time and my physical conditioning aren't what they used to be; my knees and ankles are creaking from being on my feet for hours; can I actually catch this person, or am I going to be responsible for a serious injury to one or both of us? These are some of the crazy things that go through your head at a public appearance.

Besides these swooners, these public events also feature other varieties of fans. For instance, certain females try to prove how sexy they are by attempting to seduce famous guys. Certain males try to prove their manhood by challenging you. The guys, I can handle. I have been beat up, professionally, by the best in the business, so the tough guys don't intimidate me. But the women present a problem for which I have no defense. It's not that I'm seducible. In fact, it's just the opposite. I believe in, and have always maintained, committed, faithful relationships with women. So my problem is trying to keep my distance from women who are throwing themselves at me.

Now, if you're a guy, I'm sure you're thinking I must be crazy. Beautiful women are throwing themselves at me – every man's fantasy – and I'm trying to escape? You're wondering what is my problem, right?

The problem is that if you're in a committed relationship, your wife or your girlfriend or your daughters will be watching every frame of this video. If they are with you, it creates an extremely uncomfortable situation. If the scene is replayed on social media for the whole world to see, it becomes even more embarrassing. And incidentally, it doesn't stop when you're older and paunchy and getting gray. I still get accosted – even at my 'advanced' age.

Then there are the regular fans who "just" want to chat. This is to be expected at a scheduled appearance, but is harder to tolerate when you go to a restaurant or a ball game with your kids or you try to gas up your car and people swarm around you. The "just wants" often tend to escalate to longer chats and countless autographs and selfie after selfie. And you can't just blow these people off. In the first place, that's mean. In the second place, it doesn't work. It just turns a pleasant, albeit inconvenient, exchange into an unpleasant one that will ruin the rest of everyone's day. So you just assume you're going to be late to a lot of appointments because you can be interrupted at any moment, or you just forget about 'a quiet night out' because such a thing is, at best, infrequent.

Then, on rare and unpredictable occasions, there are the accosters who are not so innocent. Some get your phone number somehow and call you incessantly. As a result, I don't answer the phone any more, not even from my friends' numbers. I call them back, or I text.

Other accosters just walk up and heap abuse and profanity on you, for God knows what reason. Maybe they feel like big shots if they dress down somebody famous. If they are drunk to boot, that really makes me nuts, because I flash back to my dad spraying beer and spit all over me when he was ranting at me as a kid.

In the extreme cases, there are the outright ambushes. I learned to keep an eye out for these at an early age. A guy came up to me in the parking lot once as I was leaving a Browns game with my family, including my 80-year-old grandmother. Nice looking guy, well dressed in a jacket and slacks. Out of nowhere he starts berating me and swearing his head off in front of my grandmother and everyone else. But I noticed that after his tirade, he slipped his hand into his jacket and looked as if he were turning on a tape recorder. So I just herded my family away from the guy and said nothing. To this day I have no idea who he was or what his agenda was. But what does it tell you when a 22-year-old is already skilled in sniffing out ambushes like that?

At one point in my playing career, my dad hired 'security' to fend off such incursions, but this was worse than being on my own. These were not the stone-faced agents with the dark sunglasses and the earbuds that you see protecting the President. No, these were typically guys my dad wanted to befriend or whom he wanted to reward or impress. All they wanted to do was rap with me constantly, so I had no peace at all. And if someone did approach, instead of shooing him off, my 'security' would turn to me and ask, "Bernie, you want me to get rid of this guy?" What am I supposed to say? I would have been better off going it alone and taking my chances.

Finally, there are the parasites. When the whole world knows your multi-million dollar salary, you might as well just tape a 'kick me' sign on your butt. For a lot of years, I was the interest-free Bank of Bernie for a whole lot of people. One good thing that came out of my filing for bankruptcy was that most of that traffic came to a screeching halt. So public bankruptcy ironically brought me some peace.

It makes you wonder why some people get so nasty in the presence of a celebrity. The parasites I get: that was pure greed and selfishness. But the ambushers and the *femme fatales* are harder for me to understand. What motivates them to hunt down celebrities and give them a hard time? Are they jealous about not being famous themselves? Do they build themselves up somehow by claiming some perverse victory over a famous person? I can't explain it, and I'm probably not qualified to. I've lived my whole adult life in a fish bowl, so it's hard for me to relate to a craving for public recognition. It was never a goal for me – it was just part of the job description. I guess some people measure their own worth by what other people think about them. I don't really get it, and it seems very sad to me.

Fortunately, those folks are in a distinct minority. The vast majority of people I meet, at fan events or just walking around, are friendly, enjoyable people. But from the twisted perspective of my own overly publicized existence, even those folks seem to have a view of celebrity that is hard for me to understand. It's like the world of fame and celebrity is some kind of parallel universe that they are not allowed into, and if they somehow get to enter it, even for a few seconds, they are like strangers in a strange land. Folks act like I'm something special, like I'm some kind of gateway into another world created by the media for 'important' people. To me, I'm just me. I feel no more important than anybody else.

Here's my point: no one needs Bernie Kosar or any other celebrity to make him or her important. Your family loves you (hopefully), even if they don't always show it. Your work is important, even if your boss doesn't always give you credit. Even if you have no family and no job, God loves you. And even if you don't believe that, believe this: your personal worth has nothing to do with your fame. Some of the most famous guys in history were ruthless, mass-murdering dictators. Plus, you know from the tabloids that the lives of many famous people are an absolute mess. My own life hasn't been so pretty at times. I can assure you that, often, life in the fishbowl is no party and anonymity is more desirable than you might realize.

I certainly have found fame and attention to be a double-edged sword. Instead of obsessing on celebrity, I think it is better to spend that energy focusing on what you have done lately for your family or your fellow humans or your own self-improvement. To me it's a total waste of time to worry about the superficial impressions you might make on people who may not even know you.

I've come to think that, on some level, people who are obsessed with celebrity lack a sense of self-confidence. As a result they turn to celebrities in an attempt to affirm their own self-worth. This is a futile effort that can't possibly provide true confidence. Confidence comes from valuing and behaving as your genuine self, not from the worship and imitation of celebrities. Confidence flows from decisions you make for yourself, not from decisions that others make for you. Confidence comes from success in personal endeavors, not from the opinions of others who barely know you. Hopefully my experiences in the limelight might inspire you to look inward (or upward) for confidence, and not outward.

Chapter 14
TRUST

You've heard a million clichés about teamwork, but none of them actually tells you what teamwork *is* – in other words – how team communication and trust actually function in a real game. I am going to break it down for you, using one of my favorite plays, which I will call the 'Rock' play. This play was my bread and butter for many years with the Browns.

The Rock play was an audible signal, in the sense that I called it at the line after seeing the defense in a particular formation. But technically it wasn't an audible because I didn't 'call' it out loud. Instead, I just held up a clenched fist (the Rock) to my receiver, and he knew exactly what to do – run deep.

The particular defensive formation that called for the Rock was tight blitz, bump-press coverage. If the weak safety cheated toward the LOS (line of scrimmage), that was even better, because that told me that the defense was focused on creating pressure, and my receiver could take off to beat the bump-press coverage (what commentators typically refer to as 'bump and run' coverage). If all worked as planned, we might connect for a TD bomb. In Cleveland Municipal Stadium, which could be a wind tunnel, I usually opted for a fade (a 25-30-yard pass) or a slant (a 6-8-yard throw) – both reasonably good gains.[19]

Some teams would apply this tight defensive coverage about 15 times a game (today, defenses are blitzing twice as much), that is, about a quarter of the time – and I would attempt to pick them apart with the Rock play

---

19 If, on the other hand, something went wrong – the weak safety recovered or my guy tripped or the cornerback didn't bite on his moves or whatever – I had various other options on the other side with my other receivers, running backs, or tight end *a la* 92 Lex Flanker Zid in Chapter 4. But for the sake of making my points about teamwork and trust, I will confine myself to the receivers.

or other audible signals. After a number of years, some of the smarter defensive coordinators wised up and called it only four or five times a game. Still, we feasted on that defense for a long, long time.

Here's where the teamwork came in. First of all, everybody knew exactly what to do, and perhaps more important, they knew what everybody else was going to do. My receiver knew, for example, that I would be looking to the right, where most of the defense was focused, to throw them off. I would not look to him until the last possible millisecond. At the same time, if I saw the weak safety closing on him, I would not throw to him. In other words, my receiver could trust me not to get him decapitated, either by giving away the play or by sending him into lethal coverage.

I, as well, knew exactly where my guy was going to be – flying down the left sideline – so I could wait until the very last millisecond to turn and release. I had to be able to trust him to be where he was supposed to be because I had to crank it up there. If my receiver was some knucklehead who decided to get creative and break off the route or cut to the inside, we have an incompletion, at best, or an interception, at worst. The announcers call this a 'miscommunication.' I call it a death sentence. If a receiver pulled that crap on me, he would never catch another pass while I was quarterback. I simply could not trust him, so I wouldn't throw him the ball.

The benefits of this trust I am talking about go deeper than just a big gainer once in a while. When things go wrong – and things do go wrong in the mayhem of a football game, just as in life – teammates don't make excuses or front off on each other. If my receiver drops the pass, even if I hit him square in the hands, I tell the post-game interviewers something like, "That incompletion was 100% my fault. I shouldn't have thrown into that coverage." By the same token, my receiver will say, "That miss was totally my fault. Bernie's pass was right there, I just couldn't grab the handle." So you could have two or three guys taking 100% responsibility for a botched play.

Trust really pays off toward the end of a game, when you are beaten up and hurt and exhausted beyond physical limits. Your typical football play may have five or six variations for the skill players, depending on how the defense sets up or reacts. Remembering what you're supposed to do in every case is hard enough when you're fresh. When your ankle is twisted or broken or your ribs are bruised or broken and maybe you've had a concussion, and you've been running your butt off and slamming into people for a few hours, it's practically impossible to keep straight all the permutations and combinations you were taught in practice. A play in which you don't have to think, where you just need to do what you've done a hundred times before – a play like that can be a godsend. But it won't work if you can't trust your teammates to do exactly what they're supposed to do, exactly like they have done it so many times before.

So what's the definition of teamwork? Everybody has a clear and simple objective. Everybody knows what's expected of him, and does it. And most important, everybody knows that everyone else will do what's expected of them. You can't do your job if you can't trust everybody else to do theirs. I can't hit my receiver if I'm wondering if he'll chicken out or space out or fail me somehow. He can't do his job if he's worried I am going to get him killed. People have to trust you to do your job, and you have to trust them to do theirs. And when it doesn't work out, you don't start pointing fingers, you cover for each other. That's how teamwork works. It's as simple as that.

Except when it isn't. In stark contrast to the pure, implicit trust I shared with certain teammates, I have to share with you a few weird tales of betrayal. And I'm not talking about family issues here, or backstabbing in the general business world. These tales are all about sports people, people I thought were like teammates.

The first relates to Art Modell, the owner of the Cleveland Browns for all the years that I was there, the same Art Modell who infamously decided in 1995 to move the team to Baltimore to become the Ravens. Although most Clevelanders regard that move as betrayal of the highest order, that's not the personal betrayal that I'm referring to.

I always had a reasonably good relationship with Modell while I was with the Browns, so when we were negotiating my contract for the '93 season, I actually gave back $1.5 million, which was about half my salary at the time, to help him out. For all the popularity of the Browns, Modell was always strapped for cash, which is ultimately why he moved the team to Baltimore. And after the '92 season, the Browns offense was pretty badly depleted, especially in the receiver department. Modell pleaded with me for some relief so he could get some good offensive free agents and start to rebuild again. It made sense to me. The quarterback is either the beneficiary or the victim of those around him. And, as you know, in my worldview, winning trumps money. So I agreed.

Modell then went out and signed a good offensive player, all right – Vinny Testeverde, my successor at the University of Miami. Modell used *my* money to acquire my replacement. How about that for betrayal?

Ok, that was business. It was deceitful and disheartening, but I get it, kind of. The betrayal that really threw me for a loop, however, was the unmasking of a man I once revered, the chaplain for the University of Miami football team, a Roman Catholic priest by the name of Leo Armbrust.

At one time Father Leo, as everybody called him, was one of my best friends in the world. In fact, he performed my wedding. I first met him as the chaplain for the U, where his unorthodox personal style earned him a rock-star reputation.

Father Leo was the furthest thing you can imagine from your stereotypical spiritual adviser. If you're thinking mild-mannered, soft-spoken Bible-quoter with a gentle, beatific smile, you've got the wrong guy, totally. Father Leo was as loud and brash and foul-mouthed and in-your-face as any football player I have ever known – in fact, far more so. He was a ball-buster *par excellence*: on the sidelines during games, in the locker room, around campus, out on the town, it didn't matter. He was constantly blasting us, joking with us, and generally trying to be one of the guys. In addition to being chaplain of the team and a regular parish priest, he hobnobbed with all kinds of local big wigs and raised serious money for Vita Nova, a home for troubled teenagers in the Miami area. Everybody loved him. I loved him. I spilled all kinds of inner secrets to the guy because I thought he was my friend. I trusted him.

Then all of *his* inner secrets began to come out. It started with accusations that he had cheated Vita Nova out of money. Then it was discovered that he had harassed some employees. Eventually he was outed as gay, which is no big deal now but was considered scandalous 20 years ago, especially for a priest. Ultimately, Father Leo had to leave the priesthood.

The revelations about the money and the harassment were pretty disturbing in and of themselves. But what upset me the most was that, in the midst of all his woes, Father Leo turned on me. I still have no idea why, other than to deflect attention from himself. He had the opportunity and the influence to squelch some nasty rumors about me, but he never did.

Instead, he told my wife and my dad and a number of important friends that he was "worried" about me, and that I was out drinking and hitting the clubs at all hours; which I was – with *him*! I was the designated driver! I was the guy hauling *him* out of bars and driving *him* home. I guess his accusations were intended to explain away his own very active nightlife, his cover story being that he was just protecting me from myself. But even if such accusations were true (which they weren't), why would he spread it all over the world? Aren't priests supposed to keep things confidential?

Here's a guy I thought was a close friend, a guy I trusted, a guy I palled around with at Miami like he was a teammate, and a Catholic priest to boot, for God's sake. It turns out he didn't trust me with anything. Even when the walls were closing in on him, he told me nothing. Instead, he turned on me. I felt like our whole relationship was a fraud.

My final tale of betrayal relates to my short-lived career in the management of the Florida Panthers hockey organization. I mentioned earlier that I became a part owner of the franchise when Wayne Huizenga sold controlling interest in 2001 to a group of local Miami businessmen. I later came to believe that one of the reasons Huizenga sold out was because he didn't want to be the one to fire club president Bill Torrey. Torrey was a legend in the NHL. He had won five Stanley Cups with the New York Islanders and had led the Panthers to the Stanley Cup finals in only their third year as an expansion franchise (1996). But things had gone downhill in the later 90's, so the new ownership group decided he had to go. Guess who eventually got elected to deliver that news to Bill?

After initially investing $4 million, and committing to a total of $6 million to the team, I was promised a position as a managing member of the club. This really appealed to me since I had just recently lost my opportunity to become a part of the Browns front office. One of my roles, along with that of David Epstein, was to serve as a public face of the organization since Alan Cohen, the majority owner, was extremely introverted and averse to the limelight. Another one of my duties, unfortunately, was to inform Bill Torrey that Alan no longer wanted him as club president.

Sensing this was coming, Bill lobbied Alan behind the scenes and convinced him to change his mind. Throughout this process, David and

I remained in the dark while Bill managed to successfully retain his role as president. As a result, I became expendable to the management team. Soon I was relieved of my executive duties and returned to passive investor status. I can only believe that I had been set up by some of my 'partners' to be the bad cop in Torrey's retirement negotiations.

So what's the lesson here? Well, one lesson is that Bernie Kosar's personal bullshit detector doesn't always work very well. I got fooled by a number of people that I had every reason to trust, so I'm clearly not the guy to tell you how to anticipate betrayal. You never hear the bullet that kills you, right?

In fact, I have come to believe that trust in your fellow man or woman isn't something you can just assume. It has to be earned. As much as I prize the trust I shared with certain long-standing teammates on the Browns, I have to admit, in retrospect, there were a lot of guys I couldn't trust. I don't mean *distrust*, like they were going to stab me in the back, or hide creepy skeletons in the closet, or steal my money, or anything like that. I just mean I couldn't *affirmatively* trust them to do their jobs. The problem might have been lack of skill, or lack of effort, or lack of focus, not necessarily selfish motivations. But the effect is like a betrayal. In the game, no trust means no team. No team means no success.

So it is in the world at large. Betrayal of trust is an ugly beast; its bite leaves a lasting scar. That's not exactly news. But I have learned to treat it like a physical injury. You can't let it knock you out of the game. You can't mistrust everybody because of one ugly situation, or even a bunch of ugly situations. You have to scramble and keep searching for the people you can trust.

I now think searching for trust is like mining for gold. There is a lot more rock in the mountain than anything precious. But if you know what you're looking for, and how to go about it, and you keep chipping away at the mountain long enough, sooner or later you're going to strike gold. And that's what trust is – the gold standard of human relationships: people you can count on to do what they're supposed to do, and who can count on you to do the same.

Chapter 15
LOVE

Don't worry, I'm not going to get all mushy on you here. God knows, I'm the last person on earth who should be giving advice on romance. My marriage was a nuclear disaster. A subsequent relationship with a well-known businesswoman fell victim to our respective, crazy travel schedules. I am in a committed relationship as of this writing, and I hope that the third time is the charm, but that hardly qualifies me as Dear Abby.

One part of love that really interests me is the word itself. We use it so much that I wonder what it really means. I love my mom. I love my kids. I love football. I love my farm. I love racing around my farm on my ATV. "I love you, bro." Obviously, I have a different relationship with my mother than I do with you or my ATV, but we use the same word for all these things. Why is that?

Let's break it down starting with Mom. Why do we all love Mom? Let's face it, part of it is because we're supposed to. Anyone who says he doesn't love his Mom has to be some kind of stone-hearted asshole, right? But also, we're grateful to Mom because she brought us up and fed us and hugged us a lot and did all kinds of things for us that we didn't care about until later life, like staying clean and dressing nicely. And just living with someone for 18 years or so breeds an intimate familiarity that you don't share with anybody else, except maybe other family members. The certainty of knowing what to expect tends to foster a sense of security. There are no surprises with Mom. Mom equals warmth and safety. We may also connect as individual personalities, which makes Mom even more lovable. But at a minimum, unless your Mom is an icicle, we all share the sense of gratitude and duty and security that are embedded in mother-love.

With your children it's entirely different. I have three girls and a boy.

So right off the bat, I have four different flavors of 'love.' Anybody with more than one kid knows what I mean. We may say, "I love all my kids just the same," but what we really mean is that we try not to rank them. I say try because when you have four different individuals, it is inevitable that your personality is going to match up differently with each one.

I'll give you an example. My girls were all into ballet, so I was obligated to attend numerous dance recitals, along with my son Joe. The two of us couldn't have cared less about the dancing, except when our girls were on stage. When they weren't, Joe and I would sneak out to goof around together on our own. We would have a ball. I did the same kind of things with my daughters, but our bond is different. Obviously, that doesn't mean I don't love my daughters just as much as Joe. It just means I love them differently.

At the same time my love for the kids is based on totally different factors than my love for Mom. They didn't raise me. I owe them no debt of gratitude. And their personalities change radically as they grow up. The stability I could count on from good old Mom is nonexistent with my kids. I never know what to expect. On the contrary I, like most parents, spend a lot of time and psychic energy just worrying about what they might be up to or into next. They scare me to death sometimes. Why is that? Why do I care so strongly about what happens to them?

I think part of it is that they are a reflection of my own success or failure as a parent. If my kids do great, well, that's because I am exceptionally gifted at fathering, right? On the other hand if that's true, then when my kids screw up and get into trouble, I must be a bad dad. I try to rationalize that it ain't necessarily so, based on my belief that my own success has little to do with my own father. So if I, and not my father, am responsible for me, why do I feel so responsible for my kids?

Rightly or wrongly, I have a lot of pride invested in how they do. And it's not just about bragging rights to their success. I want them to be happy. I feel it's my job to protect them, provide for their needs, and help them to find happiness. That's what dads are supposed to do, isn't it?

Unfortunately, I may have overdone it, just like the duty thing I discussed before. I was so eager to make my kids happy, and I had so much money when they were growing up, that I spared no expense. Everybody went to private schools. And when it came time for college, not only did I dole out full ride, out-of-state tuition, I had to make sure that they had a nice apartment and a nice car and *carte blanche* on the credit card. We all went on incredible vacations. Nobody had to get a job, but even if they did, it wouldn't provide enough money to support their lifestyles. Even worse, nobody had to mingle with the down-to-earth, less-than-privileged, working-class kids like those I grew up with in blue-collar Youngstown. My children lived in a bubble of my creation. All this I did in the name of love. So should I be shocked if any of them think they are aristocracy, and that they can do anything they damn well please, without consequences?

How is it that I could tell scary professional athletes who were bigger and stronger than I was to shut up and do what I say, when I was in the huddle, but I couldn't say no to my kids? I think the answer is that I really wanted my kids to love me, whereas in the huddle, I didn't give a damn what anybody else felt. I wanted those guys to trust me, but affection had nothing to do with it. In the game I could bitch out my best friend on the team if he screwed up, just as easily as I could bitch out some no-name rookie. On the field it was all about winning. In the family it was all about love. That was the goal. I wanted it just as badly from my kids as I wanted to win on the field, and I tried just as hard to get it.

In retrospect, however, striving so hard to get my kids to love me may have been misplaced, or even selfish. The selfish part is my own need to be loved. Maybe I have LDD (Love Deficit Disorder) because my own upbringing often seemed loveless. Maybe if I had been more Bernie the Huddle-Nazi with my kids, I could have instilled stronger values, more resilience, more determination, and a greater sense of self-reliance – all those virtues that football instilled in me. I console myself with the notion that parents have a lot less influence on their children than they like to think, and that kids are going to come out however they're going to come out, like I did. But I still beat myself up with self-doubts.

Let's get back to football. I've made it clear that I love the game. L-O-V-E with all my heart and soul. I love it so much, that after I retired from the NFL, I couldn't resist getting sucked back into arena football.

Arena football is a very different game in a number of ways. The field is about the size of a hockey rink (50 yards from goal line to goal line). There are eight players on a side, which makes for a much more wide-open game than traditional football. But the talent is pretty high caliber; hundreds of arena players have gone on to play in the NFL.

When I saw my very first game in 2008, as a guest of a friend, Jim Ferraro, who owned the Las Vegas Gladiators, I instinctively began analyzing patterns and the spacing of routes. My friend was sufficiently impressed with my analysis that he asked me to run the team, to which I readily agreed, but only on the condition that we move the team to Cleveland.

With the Cleveland Gladiators part of the fun for me was competing against former NFL rivals that were also running arena teams. John Elway ran the Denver team. Gary Fencik, captain of the Chicago Bears defense in the Buddy Ryan era, ran Atlanta. Jay Gruden, brother of Jon and former assistant coach with the Tampa Bay Buccaneers, ran the Orlando team. Ron Jaworski, former QB of the Philadelphia Eagles, ran the Philadelphia franchise, which he owned with singer Jon Bon Jovi. Competing against these guys was the next best thing to being back in the NFL. I loved it! Unfortunately, a conflict of interest cropped up with one of my other business investments, so my contract was allowed to lapse in 2013. In the meantime, however, I loved every minute of my time with the Gladiators.

But what the hell does that mean, to love a game? Part of it is physical. Winning games and winning championships, even in arena football, release a rush of endorphins that's hard to match in anything else. And of course, it's a huge ego-boost to win against the best there is.

When I was playing, as I mentioned, those little micro-victories against onrushing linebackers that were just a quarter-step too late to stop my touchdown bomb – those were euphoric for me. I also loved picking apart the blitz press coverage. You have to understand how I felt about cornerbacks pressing. I took it as a personal insult, and it enraged me. It was like they were saying my guys were pussies, and that they thought they could stop us with a little shove at the line. Webster Slaughter, Brian Brennan, and Reggie Langhorne were like my brothers. You can't insult my brothers like that. I just wanted to jam the ball up their cocky little cornerback butts. I would actually experience a moment of ecstasy when we did exactly that.

On top of everything else, it was gratifying to be able to give some joy to the long-suffering hometown fans in Cleveland during those otherwise dreary years in the 1980's. It was one of the ways I could give back to my community.

But endorphin rushes and ego boosts and self-congratulation are all selfish prizes. There is more to my love of the game than that – much more. I feel like I was made for the game, not physically, perhaps, but mentally. No mental activity grips me the way all those symbols flashing around – on the field, on the white board, on the screen – capture my fascination. It makes me feel like my greatest gift is set free to allow me to achieve my maximum potential. Even now, when all I can do is watch other people play and share some commentary, I feel like I am doing what I am *supposed* to be doing, what God put me on the earth to do. I am in laser focus. There are no doubts or fears or adversities of any kind clouding my consciousness. I comprehend everything that's going on with a clarity that I can only describe as beautiful. I am at home. I am at peace. Glory hallelujah.

OK, call me weird for using a football analogy to describe 'love.' But when you boil off all the *faux* factors, like your gratitude or sense of duty to Mom, or your self-centered pride in your children's accomplishments, or your own need for acclaim from others, what you have then distilled is a feeling not unlike what I just described. Think about it. Let's say that you know a particular human being better than anyone else in the world. Let's say you are so completely captivated by this person that everything but joy evaporates from your consciousness in their presence. Let's say this person makes you believe in and work toward the maximum potential of your own particular God-given talent, and you theirs. Let's say nothing in the world seems more meaningful to you than engaging with this person. And let's say that this person's influence suppresses all the doubts and fears and adversities in your life with a sense of peace and clarity and self-assurance. Isn't that love?

And I said I wouldn't get mushy.

Chapter 16
EVOLUTION

Needless to say, the NFL has evolved over the years, even since the era when I played. Perhaps the most obvious change has been in the athleticism of the players. Nowadays, virtually all linemen are north of 300 pounds, yet they have the agility of ballet dancers and run the 40 in 4.8 seconds. Believe me, that's fast. In my day you only saw those numbers from halfbacks and defensive backs.

In fact just using the term 'halfback' dates me. When I played running backs were divided into halfbacks and fullbacks. These terms date back to the origins of football when the backfield set up in a diamond formation behind the linemen. The guy furthest back was called the fullback (i.e., fully back). Halfway between him and the line were two 'half' backs, one on the right side and one on the left. Halfway between them and the linemen was the 'quarter' back. Get it? In those days before the modern passing game, any of these four might be the ball carrier – kind of like the wishbone offense.

By my time, of course, passing was an integral part of the game, and formations had changed accordingly. Among other things, we had the 'I' formation, in which the halfback lined up *behind* the fullback, ironically, instead of in front of him. This formation gave rise to the term 'tailback' since the halfback was now positioned at the tail of the 'I'.

So even back then the terms halfback and fullback didn't have much to do with the players' actual positions on the field anymore, but they were still meaningful. The halfbacks tended to be smaller and faster, often under six feet and 200 pounds, whereas the fullbacks tended to be somewhat bigger and beefier, at 6'2"+ and 220-240 pounds, but also a bit slower than the halfbacks.

Nowadays, we may still refer to 'scat backs' and 'power backs,' but on the whole, with the introduction of tailbacks, slot backs, blocking backs, etc., etc., etc., the distinction between halfback and fullback has virtually disappeared. That's also because nowadays, almost *all* running backs are 6'2", 230-pound bruisers who can all run 4.3 or 4.4 in the 40. Pretty amazing stuff to a guy of my vintage.

Normally, we think of evolution as something that takes place over millions of years, not 20. Obviously, something other than Darwin's theory is at work in professional football. But I hasten to add that this 'evolution' is not the work of steroids. Steroids were clearly a factor when I was playing, but the NFL has clamped down hard on these drugs, so perish that thought. Rather, the evolution is really a revolution, on a couple of fronts. One is the technology of conditioning. There are five times as many training gizmos in a modern gym as there were in my day. Also, there are multiple techniques for training specific muscle groups and various micro-skills. I recently watched a 30-minute video on improving "explosiveness," that is, the speed with which you fire off the line, or make a cut. Thirty minutes on how to improve one step? They now have virtual reality goggles to improve eye quickness. How unbelievable is that?

The other revolution is the focus on diet and body chemistry. In my era we ate pretty much whatever we felt like. Most players didn't think twice about nutrition. The most sophisticated supplement we ever had was Gatorade[20] (other than the training room pain killers and anti-inflammatories described in Chapter 2). Nowadays, dedicated players are virtual food scientists whose diets are as regimented as their practice schedules. They know all the nutrients (or toxins) in every type of food, and they know exactly what they have to eat and in what proportions, along with what foods they need to avoid.

All this science has produced remarkable improvements in player size, strength, and speed in a relatively short period of time, and, for the most part, without the use of dangerous drugs. Furthermore, the eager adoption

---

20 A lot of the development of this product took place in conjunction with the football team of the University of Florida (hated rivals of my own Miami Hurricanes), hence the name 'Gator-ade.' To this day, Florida reaps some $12 million a year in royalties for its role.

of all this science and technology by the players tells me that the 'winning is the only thing' mentality is still alive and well in the NFL. Very few people would put themselves through the agony of all these exotic new exercises and drills and food disciplines just to stay fit. You have to be committed to a goal.

I also recognize that the goal we are talking about here carries the promise of mega-riches. Clearly, the big money factors into this motivation. But you don't get the big money unless you out-compete all the other tens of thousands of guys trying to get into the NFL; and you're not going to out-compete them unless you dedicate maximum effort to preparation. So I would argue that the phenomenal economic success of the League has also contributed to this revolution in the athleticism of players.

The same quantum improvement in players, however, cannot necessarily be observed in the non-playing personnel involved in the game. You have already read my homily about front office suits who are more concerned with office politics than winning football games. I also worry that big money may be having a distracting effect on some of the coaches and scouts and other supporting cast members as well. I exclude the head coaches from this discussion because they are the top dogs of field management and have always been relatively well-compensated. I'm talking about staff members further on down the food chain. For purposes of brevity, I will pick on assistant coaches as the prime example, but the argument can apply to many others in the ranks who have become far more prominent nowadays than they ever were in my day. I wonder about the effects that big money and newfound fame are having on their attitudes and decision-making.

In the past assistant coaches were a dime a dozen. Teams paid these guys like working stiffs, maybe $35,000 per year, and treated them like interchangeable parts. If an assistant coach looked at the wrong guy cross-eyed, boom, he was gone, and somebody else was quickly and easily brought in.

If you happened to be one of those coaches, getting canned every year or two had serious personal consequences. You had to move the family, sell the house, buy a new one (all on $35k), and stick the kids in new schools all the time. So you played it straight. You stuck to your knitting. You focused on doing your job and getting the best out of your assigned group of players. Basically, you were a blue collar Joe Lunchbucket, regardless of how brilliant you were. Generally speaking, assistant coaches were nameless guys that kept low profiles because, well, the hammer comes down on the nail that's sticking out the most.

Enter the agents. In the mid-80's, agents had a light-bulb moment. It dawned on them that, whereas the average player had a career lifespan of three to five years, a coach might stay employed for 30 or more. If an agent could get his annual piece of that action, he would have an annuity. So agents began recruiting coaches as clients and replicated the techniques that had worked so well to elevate player pay. Neil Cornrich, a Cleveland-based agent whom I always wanted to work with, was a brilliant pioneer of this technique.

In the process pay jumped to six or seven digit contracts with multi-year guarantees for coordinators, top assistants, and front office personnel. Now it was a lot more costly for teams to throw coaches overboard. Also, from the coaches' points of view, they weren't so worried about getting fired. If you have a five-year deal, getting axed after two isn't so bad. That leaves three years to hit the beach, or go get another six or seven-digit gig and double-dip for a while.

The agent-coach relationship had other mutual benefits besides more money for both parties. Players who had aspirations to play for particular teams could be more easily recruited by agents who also represented coaches of those teams. This was good for the agents' business. At the same time, agents could help coaches attract particular players that the coaches desired for their squad. Obviously, the team that paid the most money would have the inside track for any particular sought-after player. But all else being equal, economically, wouldn't a player rather play for a team where his agent had an influential relationship with the coaching staff and/or front office personnel?

This 'Rise of the Assistant Coach' has had some other interesting effects. As their pay has risen, so has their status. They are now personalities, if not exactly celebrities. Media people seek them out for comment and insight, and some coaches are all too happy to oblige, sometimes with 'off-the-record' interviews, but often times with on-camera appearances. They dig the attention. Who doesn't love being seen on TV by his mom and his kids? It's cool, right? Plus, it creates an appearance of importance.

Such attention, however, can have unfortunate consequences. In an effort to please the media, assistant coaches can inadvertently reveal critical information. Perhaps they tip their hand about team strategy in an upcoming game, or about the availability of a key player who is in 'questionable' status. Such revelations can be very helpful to the opposition. Head coaches are well practiced in the arts of evasion and deception in a press conference (e.g., Bill Belichick), but assistant coaches who are eager to enhance their brand and marketability by cozying up to the media are not always so careful.

I also worry when I see an interview with an assistant who is dressed up too sharply and groomed like a TV star. As I said, I'm used to old-school, working Joes in smelly old grey sweats. So when I see a Ken Doll on TV, I wonder how much time was spent getting pretty, as opposed to watching film or working with staff or doing the sorts of things that win football games. Maybe I'm an old relic, but it makes me queasy.

To be clear, I am not condemning all assistant coaches by any means. Certainly the top teams are staffed with excellent people who have the focus, the work ethic, and the winning attitude that you have to have to be successful in the NFL. Again, I am not criticizing assistant coaches, alone. Where a problem exists, front office people, scouts, and others often share the blame. However, I am disturbed by how this growing trend of publicity and exposure seems to be more important – and profitable – than winning.

Back to the players. For me, personally, one of the most fascinating evolutions in today's game is the emergence of the running quarterback – given my own limitations in that department. Throughout football history there have always been quarterbacks who could run; in fact, that's what the position entailed, originally. And certainly in my era, a few quarterbacks were noted for their legs. Fran Tarkenton was famous for his mad scrambles. And of course, John Elway plagued my Browns teams, repeatedly, with his quick-footed ability to elude tacklers and make a big gain out of a disaster. Randall Cunningham also had hot wheels.

However, during my era, speed was basically a way for a QB to get out of trouble. Running plays were not designed for quarterbacks, even for quarterbacks who could run. Since about 2010, however, things have changed noticeably. In recent years we have seen the emergence of super-athletic quarterbacks – so-called 'dual threats' – for whom running is a regular, live option.

The ability of running quarterbacks has led to a change in the passing game. Old school 'pocket passers' like me dropped back and read the activity downfield, looking deep first, then middle, then, if all else failed, short. I rarely called some dinky short pass in the huddle. I was always thinking bomb; but I also made a lot of money in the intermediate zone, meaning 12-18-yard routes.

That zone seems to have vanished for the dual-threat quarterbacks. If they aren't running, they are throwing really quick outs or screens. Or, if they are going long, they are doing it on the run. In other words, they throw right away, or they run around for a few seconds while the receivers get downfield. That style basically rules out the intermediate passing game. The absence of intermediate passing options also subverts the deep game.

This approach may work fine in high school and college, if the quarterback is physically head-and-shoulders above everyone else on the field. In the NFL, however, I just don't believe it's consistently effective, particularly at playoff time. For one thing the talent level of the defensive players is a league above, literally, what exists in high school or college. You can't just outrun these guys like you might have before; and if they catch you and clock you, it's going to hurt.

For another thing the blocking skills of the linemen are not going to progress like you need them to by playoff time. Recall how I needed my guys to hold blocks for three to four seconds. If they never have to do that in the regular season because the quarterback is always moving around, they won't be able to do it in the playoffs when they are facing the best of the best.

Now you might say, "But Bernie, look at Cam Newton and Russell Wilson. They did great in the playoffs." To which I would respond by saying that Cam Newton and Russell Wilson have evolved into pretty good pocket passers, even though they still rack up the rushing yardage. They think 'pass' first and second, and generally think 'run' only as a third option when they're forced to.

More important, however, I would point to all the dual threat flameouts that have occurred since 2010. I give you Tim Tebow, who after his miracle half-season with Denver in 2011, was traded away and ultimately disappeared into the minor league baseball system of the New York Mets. I give you Robert Griffin III, aka RG3, who was NFL offensive Rookie of the Year with the Redskins in 2012, but by 2015 was their third string quarterback. After the 'Skins cut him in 2016, the Browns gave him a shot, but he broke his shoulder in week one of the 2016 season, was out for most of the year, and was finally released in early 2017. I give you Colin Kaepernick, who also got off to a great start in 2012 and 2013, then went 8-8 in 2014, lost his starting job in 2015, was released in 2016, and as of this writing, is still trying to latch onto a team. And then of course, we have the sad case, noted earlier, of Johnny Manziel, "Johnny Football" at Texas A&M, who never really made it out of the starting blocks after two seasons with the Browns.

Do you see a pattern here? We have four QB's who were lights out in college, three of whom were also phenomenal for a year or two in the pros. But within a few years, all were riding the bench. What do you suppose happened?

I have already suggested a partial answer: the dual-threat quarterback is less and less threatening as the competition becomes more and more intense. But it is also true that a running quarterback just can't survive as long in the NFL. Running backs in the NFL have an average career span of 3.11 years, the shortest of any position, because they take so much punishment. If you turn quarterbacks into running backs, you're likely to shorten their careers to a similar level. Injuries were the downfall of RG3. Ditto Kaepernick, who had shoulder surgery a week after he lost his starting job. This is true of Manziel as well, who racked up a bunch of injuries in his short stint with the Browns (admittedly, he had other issues as well).

I suspect that the League is falling out of love with the dual threat quarterback because of all these high profile failures. Among the top teams you will see – and are seeing – a return to old school pocket passing. But a question remains: how did this state of affairs come about in the first place? Wasn't it obvious that deliberately exposing quarterbacks to the run would shorten their careers?

No doubt one reason for the infatuation with dual-threat QB's was the added excitement of play. A guy who can throw *and* run is like Superman, and we all want to see what he can do. Excitement is also enhanced by the risk of running the quarterback because the stakes are so high. If he gets laid out while darting through the minefield, well, it could be 'Game Over,' or even 'Season Over.' So fans hold their breath when the QB takes off.

However, I can't help wondering whether coaches didn't tilt toward this style of play because it simplified their lives. If you have the running QB, you don't need to worry so much about that intermediate passing game; your completion stats will look strong enough with all the little dink passes that any quarterback could complete. So why sweat all those complicated routes and blocking schemes that take so much preparation and practice time? We already have too much on our plates as it is. After all, we have to attend to our media relations, and intelligence-sharing with our agents, and all our other career advancement activities (Sorry – I couldn't help myself). This is a trend, in my humble opinion, which too closely resembles the self-serving behavior of certain front office suits that I lamented earlier.

I want to emphasize that this trend is not League-wide. As I said before, you're unlikely to find any distracted people in the top organizations – the ones that are totally dedicated to the idea that winning is the only thing. However, while everyone might say that, saying it and actually doing the things that it takes to win are completely different. What disturbs me is the prevalence of only 'talking the talk' in many of the unsuccessful organizations. As a result, I fear that the vaunted parity of the NFL is giving way to a growing spread between the winners and the losers.

"Parity in jeopardy?" you ask. Between 2011 and 2015, we have had five different Super Bowl winners. Isn't that parity?

To which I say, take a deeper dive into the numbers. In those same five seasons, three teams had winning percentages over .700 (New England, Denver, and Green Bay). Four more teams had winning percentages over .600 (Seattle, Cincinnati, Pittsburgh, and San Francisco). Taken together, those seven teams (about 20% of the League) had a combined winning percentage of .675. In the same five-year period, those seven teams collectively played in 30 playoff games, including seven Super Bowl appearances.

Now look at the other end of the spectrum. Four teams had winning percentages below .300 (Cleveland, Tampa Bay, Tennessee, and Jacksonville) and three teams were below .400 (Washington, St. Louis, and Oakland). Collectively, they had a winning percentage of .305, which translates into four or five wins per year, against 11 or 12 losses, every year for five years. Of these seven teams, five never had a winning season the entire time. None of the seven ever appeared in a playoff game in five years.

Is that parity, or parody? Seven teams win over two-thirds of their games (New England is over three-quarters), and seven teams can't average one-third (Jacksonville can't manage one quarter). If I showed you these numbers with no team names or cities, you'd think I was talking about the NBA, right?

Dynasties are not new to the NFL: Lombardi's Packers, Noll's Steelers of the 70's. Why, even the Cleveland Browns were a dynasty back in the Paul Brown era. It was easier then because free agency didn't exist, for all practical purposes. A team could hang on to its stars for as long as it wanted.

Once free agency came along top players could go where the money was. But the money is pretty equally distributed in the NFL, thanks to salary cap restrictions and the communal sharing of TV revenue. As a result, you don't have 'rich' teams that can snap up all the talent, like you do in baseball. Teams can make some strategic acquisitions, and they do that, but not to an overwhelming extent. So free agency created a much more fluid situation and actually helped to promote parity in the League for many years by distributing the talent fairly equally.

Parity, in turn, helped feed the popularity of the sport because fans could justifiably believe that with a decent draft and a couple of key acquisitions, their team had a fighting chance. No opponent, no matter how fearsome, could monopolize stars for very long, so there was always hope. And hope breeds higher attendance and TV ratings.

So if we don't have indentured servitude of players anymore, and no one can buy up all the talent, how then do we wind up with the current dynastic situation? I believe the answer comes down to management – or mismanagement. When the front offices and coaching staffs and support personnel have the 'winning is everything' commitment – with action, and not just words – along with the talent to go with it, their teams will rule. If not – if individual ambitions and personal enrichment trump the collective goal of the team – those teams will continue on the losing path.

There is irony in this re-stratification of the NFL. As pro football has become more and more popular, the money involved has gotten bigger and bigger. This big money seems to have bred better talent on the field, but at the same time, seems to have distracted some of the supporting cast members from their all-consuming focus on winning football games.

This trend may not be League-wide, but it has League-wide consequences. If a quarter of the League drops out of contention permanently, what happens to the audiences in those markets? And if the audience shrinks, what happens to the TV revenue, not to mention the gate in the forlorn cities, and the merchandise sales and the sponsorship fees, and all the other ancillary income? In other words I wonder whether the temptation of big money has distorted incentives to the point that revenue could actually fall. I wonder if the NFL has become so successful that it could now be eroded by its own success.

Funny how evolution works, isn't it?

Chapter 17
PERSPECTIVE

I recently witnessed an interesting phenomenon. As you probably know, on June 19, 2016, the Cleveland Cavaliers won the first championship in their 47-year history, and the first championship in NBA history in which the winner battled back from a 3-1 deficit, with native son LeBron James leading the charge. What you probably don't know is that by the following evening, you couldn't buy a copy of *The Plain Dealer*, Cleveland's major daily, for love nor money, anywhere in town, even though the newspaper had printed three times the normal number. Every available copy had been bought up by the townspeople as mementos of the Cavaliers glorious victory in the NBA Finals. This victory ended a championship drought – known to locals as The Curse – that dated back to the Browns' last NFL Championship in 1964.

With that gorilla off our back, I think it is high time to put The Cleveland Curse into some historical perspective. As one who personally suffered through The Drive and The Fumble, two of the most excruciating episodes of The Curse, I have had a long time to ruminate about this, and about the outsized impact sports have on our civic life.

For those of you who are not Cleveland sports fans and have no idea what I am talking about, check out the ESPN *30 for 30* special titled *Believeland*, which documents The Cleveland Curse in all its gory details. There is an old version and a newer one which ESPN produced after the Cavaliers' 2016 Championship. Either one will paint the whole, ugly, bloody picture for you.

The Drive to which I refer occurred in the AFC Championship played on January 11, 1987, in Cleveland, the weekend after our magnificent double-overtime comeback win over the Jets. In The Drive game John

Elway and the Denver Broncos took the ball from their own two-yard line, with less than five minutes to play, and drove 98 yards to tie the game and force overtime, which they won with a field goal.

The Fumble refers to the last offensive play we ran against the same Denver Broncos in the 1988 AFC Championship game, played on January 17 in Denver. Near the end of this game, our running back Earnest Byner lost control of the ball on the Denver two-yard line with a minute left as we were driving for what would have been the game-tying touchdown. Instead, Denver recovered the ball, killed the clock by taking a last-second safety, and we lost, 38-33. You can still see The Fumble on YouTube, as this play has become an NFL legend.

Sadly, The Drive and The Fumble have become part of a long-standing narrative of tragic defeats in Cleveland sports history, including:

Red Right 88 (January 4, 1981): In a divisional championship against the Oakland Raiders, the Kardiac Kids, as the Browns were known in the Brian Sipe era, took possession at their own 15 yard line, down by two points with 2:22 left on the clock. They marched 57 yards in a minute and 26 seconds to the Oakland 28. But instead of kicking the field goal, Head Coach Sam Rutigliano, worried that his normally trusty kicker Don Cockroft was injured (and had already missed two field goals), called for a pass play, Red Right 88. The Raiders intercepted in the end zone and won the game, 14-12.

The Shot (May 7, 1989): In a preview of his championship career to come, young Michael Jordan took an inbounds pass with three seconds left in the deciding first-round playoff game against the heavily-favored Cleveland Cavaliers. He beat a double-team, and with Craig Ehlo's hand flashing across his face, lofted the winning basket just before the buzzer. The Cavs lost, 101-100.

Game 7 (October 26, 1997): In Game 7 of the 1997 World Series against the Florida Marlins, Cleveland Indians closer Jose Mesa blew a one-run lead in the bottom of the ninth inning. The Marlins went on to score the winning run in the 11th, costing the Tribe its first World Series since 1948.

As an aside, I happened to witness this loss personally, since I had been given behind-the-dugout seats by Marlins owner Wayne Huizenga, my business partner in the Florida Panthers. If you find video of the winning hit, you will see my mom and me in the background as Craig Counsell triumphantly prances around third headed for home with the winning run. You will also notice that I do not look as happy as a guest of the Marlins owner ought to be in that situation because obviously I was rooting for the Tribe.

The common theme in all these episodes is a late-game mishap that kept a Cleveland team from advancing to, or winning, the championship. As you can see, it's not just the Browns. The Cavs and Indians have also been victimized. Together, these stories combine in the popular imagination to make up the Cleveland Curse, a narrative worthy of Greek tragedy. The gods have condemned us to eternal failure. We are considered a city of losers.

This last idea is completely crazy in my opinion. All of the Cleveland teams we are talking about here were great teams, including, if I may say so, the two that I was on. They all had impressive winning records in their regular seasons, they all won their divisions, and except for The Shot, they all won their early round playoffs. They were all phenomenally talented teams. But a lot of people in Cleveland refuse to see the glass as 95% full. It always looks 5% empty.

And it's not just Cleveland. In America in general, we divide the sports world into the champions, and everybody else. If you're the champion, you're a hero. If you're not, you're a loser. Really? We don't do this in any other sphere of activity. Because Bill Gates is the richest man in America, does that make Warren Buffet a loser? I bet Warren doesn't think so.

So why do we obsess about champions in sports and write off all other contenders as worthless? My own theory is that our society has a tendency to use sports as a substitute for warfare. In war there is no second place. In war you either win or you die, or at a minimum, your world is reduced to rubble. It doesn't matter how many battles you've won before, or whom you've beaten. If you lost the last battle, you are a loser in the worst sense of the word.

Now maybe you're thinking, "Bernie, c'mon. War? Seriously? It might have *felt* like war down on the playing field, with gigantic men chasing you around and mauling your body and slamming you to the ground. But it's not like they had guns and knives. In fact there's even a penalty for 'unnecessary roughness,' isn't there? How is that like war?"

By no means am I saying that it's war in the actual sense. And I am in no way comparing myself or my teammates to real warriors, our brave soldiers in uniform who sacrifice so much for us. I have friends who were in the Army Rangers and Seal Team 6. I have friends who are Vietnam veterans who are still suffering from the effects of Agent Orange. I have nothing but infinite respect for those guys. I am not saying sports experiences are even close to what they went through.

What I am saying is, for the fans, sports serve as an outlet for the warrior instincts that are part of our DNA. I didn't originate this idea. It's been with us since the first Olympics in ancient Greece, and scholars have been debating it for years. But here's my take.

Mankind has been around for hundreds of thousands of years. We know for a fact that there have been wars virtually non-stop throughout history, including those occurring right now. And it's pretty safe to assume that even before recorded history, cavemen were killing each other as soon as they could stand up straight. So for hundreds of thousands of years, we have been adapting to warfare – for food, for defense, for whatever reason. We are a warrior species.

Now in the course of history, we have also learned that war is horrible and self-destructive, and we have taken steps to avoid it. We haven't had a World War in 70 years now, although clearly there are smaller wars going on at this very moment. But even though countries have managed to avoid major wars with each other in recent decades, you don't wipe out thousands of years of evolution in two or three generations. Those instincts that kept us alive all that time are still there; we've just learned to control them a little better.

One way we control our warrior instincts is through sports. Sports let us express some of that innate aggression in non-lethal doses. And I'm not talking only about the players here, I'm talking about the fans. And it's not just football. Fans get just as crazy at big moments in baseball games, basketball games, or hockey games. In fact hockey fans may take the cake for crazy. People who are calm, friendly, law-abiding citizens in normal life, often go berserk at sporting events. That's why they go, or watch on TV. They want to see the aggression, the fight-to-the-death effort, the hard hitting (whether it's a ball or a puck or another human being), and ultimately, the victory. Avid fans may be into the strategy and tactics and statistics of the game, but at the end of the day, they want to scream their heads off, too.

NASCAR is an extreme example of what I'm talking about. It is said that NASCAR fans go to see the wrecks, not the races. I don't know if that's true or not, but it is true that NASCAR drivers are living on the brink of death every moment they are on the track. The constant threat of death in an intense, high-speed competition – sounds a little like war, doesn't it?

Or think about the WWE. It is designed to present maximum violence and ferocity. Wrestlers jump on each other, throw each other out of the ring, and smash each other with chairs, all the while bellowing like wild animals. It is staged to look like hand-to-hand combat, and even though fans know it's staged, they get into it like it was the real thing. They bellow just as loudly as the wrestlers. It's like a primal scream on a massive scale.

So this is how we, as a society, blow off steam. We go to games and we scream and we holler with all our might, like we ourselves were locked in pitched battle. This impedes the aggressive passions in our make-up from building up and exploding into real war.

As a method of letting some steam out of the global pressure cooker, sports are a positive thing. But the corollary is that we forget it's a game and act like sports is war. So when our team loses, we are devastated. The bigger the game, the more intense the devastation. Though our team may have a great record, or win the division or advance in the playoffs – none of that matters to us. We lost the war. We're crushed. We're chumps. We're losers. We'd rather be dead.

That's how fans react. Players even more so. I joke with my friends in the military that they might be the lucky ones: if they screw up, they won't be around to deal with the consequences. Players, on the other hand, have to live with their mistakes and the public humiliation that goes with it, forever. A lot of my teammates on those '86 and '87 Browns teams would rather have died than lose those AFC championship games. God knows, I myself wanted to crawl in a hole and die.

This is the magnifying glass through which we view professional sports. And as every little kid knows, if you hold the magnifying glass just right in the sun and concentrate the sun's rays, you can set something on fire. This is what happened to my teammate Earnest Byner as a result of The Fumble.

I have to delve into The Fumble, painful as it is for long-time Browns fans, for a few reasons. First of all, I'm the guy who handed off the ball that

Earnest fumbled, so I had a ringside seat that very few other people had. Second, I want to make a larger point about human nature, which I'll get to later. But finally, I have to set the record straight for the benefit of my teammate and good friend.

Earnest will never do this. From the time of the post-game press conference after The Fumble to this very day, Earnest has done nothing but man up and take 100% responsibility for ending the Browns' playoff hopes in the 1987 season. He has never made any excuses; he has never fronted off on any teammates; he has never tried to downplay the significance of The Fumble, and he never will. That would be a violation of his personal code of honor. Instead, he told the press, "I should have tucked it in more." In the opening chapter of his own book, Earnest states, "I squarely put the loss of the [1987] AFC Championship Game on my shoulders."[21]

Sorry, bro, but that's bullshit. I was right there, and I know what happened. The first thing everybody needs to remember is that The Fumble did NOT lose the game. We were already losing by a touchdown (38-31), with only a minute to go. Had Byner scored, we would have only tied the game (assuming we didn't mess up the conversion), and we would have gone into overtime. Who knows what would have happened in OT? It's not like the Broncos were some kind of slouch team.

The next thing everybody needs to remember is that Byner not only had a good overall game, he had an unbelievable second half. As a team we stunk up the joint in the first half. We fumbled and turned the ball over a bunch of times. Nobody remembers that. We were down 21-3 at halftime. I was so mad at halftime that I blew up in the locker room and told a bunch of my teammates that I had had it with the game plan and the chicken-shit play calls, and I was going to take things over.

Then we caught fire and scored 21 points in the third quarter. Byner scored two of those three touchdowns. Then, in the fourth quarter, he caught a pass for 53 yards that set up the touchdown that tied the game at 31. Byner had 187 total yards, mostly in the second half, which was more than twice as many as any other back or receiver in the whole game. Without Earnest Byner, we never get to The Fumble. We get our butts whipped in a very forgettable game.

Then there's the play itself, which I called. My decision to call a running

---

21 *Everybody Fumbles* (EB21 Productions: 2015), p. 10.

play, ironically, was based on misgivings that haunted me about The Drive a year earlier. The go-ahead touchdown we scored just before The Drive was a 48-yard bomb to Brian Brennan. Part of me says if you have a chance to score, you have to score. But part of me knows full well that my bomb left a lot of time on the clock for Elway and company, which they used to kill us. So I was determined to leave them as little time as possible in this rematch. We would run the ball and eat up some clock. If Earnest didn't make it in, we'd run it again and eat up some more clock.

The play I called is designed to go through the seven hole (outside the left tackle), with the right guard, Dan Fike, pulling out to lead the runner through the hole. Paul Farren, our left tackle, washed the defensive end to the inside, as he was supposed to, so Fike plowed to the outside with Byner behind.

At this point Byner was cradling the ball in his left arm, as he should have, to protect it from the 10 guys who were chasing him from the right. Unfortunately, the one guy to his left, Broncos right corner Jeremiah Castille, was not blocked. Earnest realized this but headed for the end zone anyway, figuring Denver hadn't stopped him all day. Castille, however, flailed and punched the ball out of Byner's left arm, and the rest you know.

As far as the missed block is concerned, Earnest would never call out a teammate, and neither will I. But our Head Coach Marty Schottenheimer had no such reluctance: "[Name withheld] is supposed to take 10 steps upfield, then block Castille to the outside. Instead, he watched the play." Offensive Line Coach Howard Mudd expressed a similar sentiment: "One of our guys was lazy and the Broncos dumbed into the fumble and the Super Bowl trip."

'Lazy' is too harsh. After 59 minutes of championship football, you are beyond exhausted. As I said at the outset, you are way past the Wall of Pain. You are completely drained. Nearly dead maybe, but *not* lazy. In the case of the blocking receiver in question, I had sent the poor guy on so many deep routes in the second half that it was a miracle he could even stand up. There is no question he left it all on the field that day.

Byner's condition was hardly better. On the play before The Fumble, I had sent him on a 40-yard pass route, and because we were running out of time, he had to hustle 40 yards back. So he was still sucking wind in the huddle. But nobody talks about that or The Missed Block. They talk about The Fumble. There were all kinds of other mix-ups and mess-ups I could recount from that game. Hell, I myself threw an interception (with an oily ball!). Nobody talks about The Interception. So why The Fumble?

The obvious answer is that The Fumble was the final miscue that ended our last chance to save the game. In that instance hope died. Hope died for our team and for all the Browns fans who were rooting for us. Earnest was our last, best hope, and he lost the ball. So he became the villain, the guy blamed for killing hope for everybody.

I personally never subscribed to this. When Earnest was on the field, I always felt we had hope. But immediately after The Fumble, Earnest was like Hiroshima after the bomb, sitting alone in silence, surrounded by a wide radius of emptiness, devastated and radioactive. No one wanted to go near him. I went over to hug him and give him some love, for whatever that was worth. But there was no consoling him. He felt like the assassin of hope.

When I think about Earnest and The Fumble, I sometimes think about Moses in the Bible. Moses, as you know, stood up to the Pharaoh and said "Let my people go," at a time when you could get your head chopped off for attitude like that. Then, when God gave the all-clear, Moses rounded up his people and led them out of Egypt. What kind of stones did that take, to walk through a tunnel in the sea that could collapse on you and drown you at any second? Then he led his people through the wilderness for 40 years, living on nothing but manna from Heaven. Forty years! But after all that, Moses never made it to the Promised Land. He died on the east bank of the Jordan as his people were poised to cross over. He could see it, but he couldn't touch it. Do we say Moses fumbled? Do we call him a loser or a choke because he didn't cross the goal line? No. We revere him as one of the great leaders in history.

Earnest Byner led his team through all kinds of adversity, withstood all kinds of physical punishment, and rose up to all kinds of difficult challenges. Like Moses, he never 'crossed the goal line' either in Cleveland, but history didn't revere him as a hero. History made him into Public Enemy #1. Public opinion nailed him to a cross.

Afterward, Earnest spent more than three days in Hell. The Fumble plagued him for years. It was at least 10 years before he could even talk about it. Since then, he has come to terms with it, accepted it, and even written about it. But to this day fans come up to him and say things like, "Don't fumble!" Can you believe some people think that's funny?

Psychologists talk about various stages of grief. The first stage is denial, which we got through after that championship game in less than a minute. There was no denying we lost.

The next stage is anger, and Earnest Byner became the focus of that anger for many fans.[22] But the issue wasn't really Byner. Like I said, if you analyze the game rationally, he was a big reason we were even in it at the end. The issue is human nature, like the sports-as-war thing. Human nature tends to react to a painful loss with anger. That anger has to go somewhere, and in this case, the magnifying glass of big-time sports focused its intensity on the guy who "killed hope," in many fans' perception – hope that wouldn't even have been possible without his enormous contribution. Talk about a victim of his own success.

Eventually, grief morphs into the depression stage, and Cleveland has been wallowing in that for a long, long time. But ultimately, the mourner comes to the final stage: acceptance. I hope that the perspective I have provided here helps those who are still obsessing about The Fumble to snap out of it. It's been 30 years, people. It's time to move on.

I have to share one last Byner anecdote that goes to the question of acceptance. In 2015, at the very time the Cleveland Cavaliers were playing Golden State for the NBA Championship the first time, Earnest and I were at a fan event in Dayton, Ohio. The two of us were sitting at a table signing autographs, with a big-screen TV in full view showing a pre-game feature on The Cleveland Curse – The Fumble, The Drive, The Shot, the whole works – over and over again on a loop. Earnest was forced to watch The Fumble at least five or six times while we were sitting there. There was no way to escape it. Earnest was quiet and composed, but I could see the emotion all over his face. Thanks for that, ESPN.

The point here is that Earnest Byner has become so much more than a symbol for a tragic loss. He has become a model for facing scorn of

---

22 While scorn for Byner is all too widespread in Cleveland, it is not universal. Those who saw the 2016 ESPN special *Believeland* witnessed the loving reception he got from devoted fans at the end of the last game played in Cleveland Municipal Stadium by the old Browns, where Earnest finished his career after a very successful interlude with the Washington Redskins.

the cruelest kind, and overcoming it. For one thing, after being traded by Cleveland to Washington, he helped the Redskins to their Super Bowl victory in 1992 and finally won the ring he so rightly deserved.

So I believe it is high time for all Clevelanders to look at Earnest in a new light. He has taken an excruciating event and turned it into an opportunity, not only to win a Super Bowl ring, but also to teach others about dealing with adversity, both through his coaching career and in his book, *Everybody Fumbles*. His book is addressed primarily to football players and coaches, but even the general reader will find nuggets of wisdom about confronting setbacks, learning from mistakes, and other techniques of 'scrambling.' I recommend it to everyone for those reasons, but also to see how Cleveland's sacrificial lamb has transformed himself into a mentor.

In my book Earnest has overcome the media torture which misplaced public anger subjected him to for so many years. In my book he has become a symbol of transcendence and resurrection as a result of his stoicism and resilience. And if you watch *Believeland*, with the revised ending that ESPN produced after the Cav's 2016 championship victory, Earnest looks and talks like a man who has been redeemed and reborn.

So maybe now that the Cavs have lifted Cleveland out of its 50-year funk over the stupid Curse, we can put Byner's saga into proper perspective. Maybe we can put our whole attitude about sports into proper perspective and acknowledge a little remorse over the extreme collateral damage of our sports mania. It's a game, folks. It's supposed to be fun to watch. It's not *really* war.

Chapter 18
RESILIENCE

You already know my personal history with concussions. In my lifetime concussions in football have gone from a non-issue no one even thought about; to a festering concern that the NFL denied for a long time; to a grave problem that the League is now addressing attentively. I am confident that the League will come up with beneficial changes – better equipment, new rules, new technology, improved treatments – not just for humanitarian reasons, but because the hazard of concussions presents an existential threat to the sport. It jeopardizes not only the handsome livings earned by those in the football world, but also the enormous profits grossed in the media and business worlds. Already, worried parents are pulling their kids out of the sport. The concussion issue is now fair game for PBS *Frontline* specials and a feature length movie starring Will Smith (who pulled *his* son out of football). The game is currently under attack.

I worry about where this assault will lead. I say *worry* because, first of all, I'm not sure we are asking the right questions. The public controversy seems to be focused on whether there is a link between football and head injuries, to which I say, "Duh!" I don't think you have to be a doctor or a scientist to figure out that one. When you have several hundred of the world's largest and strongest athletes smashing into each other as hard as possible several dozen times a game for years on end, odds are injuries – some severe, some permanent – will occur to every part of the human anatomy, head included. To me, this is a blinding flash of the obvious, like "Is there a link between driving cars and car accidents?" The point here is that we are focused on a question that is no longer *in* question, instead of addressing questions that could lead to productive answers.

A logical first question is, "How bad is the problem?" Chronic traumatic encephalopathy (CTE) is a nasty malady; so nasty that some of its victims, including guys I knew in the game, committed suicide rather than endure the misery. And these guys were as tough as they come. I knew Andre Waters, for example, from the very first American Bowl played at Wembley Stadium in England, between the Browns and the Philadelphia Eagles. He had a rough reputation in the League, and he and I fought for the whole week leading up to the game, in pubs and anywhere else in London where we ran into each other. In 2006, 11 years after his retirement, he killed himself with a shotgun.

I knew Dave Duerson from similar battles, first in college when we fought in the tunnel before a game between the Hurricanes and Notre Dame, and then again in 1986, when Duerson was with the Chicago Bears. In 2011, Dave shot himself in the chest, specifically so that his brain could be sent to Boston University for study, which confirmed that he did in fact have CTE.

I also knew Junior Seau personally. I got a call from him in April 2012, during which he told me how bad his head hurt. I remember that call vividly because five days later, he too shot himself, also in the chest, like Duerson, so that his brain could be examined. A study by the National Institutes of Health (NIH) concluded that he, too, suffered from CTE.

When that many guys you know – guys with whom you had close personal contact – kill themselves because their suffering is so intense, you recognize that CTE is not some remote, abstract problem. It is real and personal and horrifying. From my own head trauma, I know something about constant splitting headaches and insomnia and other debilitating problems. What these guys – all of them tough as nails – went through, I can only imagine.

At the same time most players haven't died of CTE, so we need to look into why some suffer and some don't. Is there a genetic factor we can screen for? Are other factors involved? A number of the players who've died from CTE played in the era when steroids were rampant. Some players, let's be honest, were party animals. Could substance abuse be a factor?

I don't know the answers to these questions. Other people more qualified than I am are looking into it. But one thing that is probably safe to say is that the incidence of CTE in former NFL players is significantly higher than in the population at large, and that fact alone should be enough to make us ask what we can do about it.

The answer to this question has several branches. One branch, as suggested above, is diagnostics that might help us screen out people with a propensity for CTE. That's going to take a lot of research, which is just beginning to get underway. Another branch is technological innovations that either make the game safer or the diagnosis better. In this regard a variety of innovations are being explored, ranging from more forgiving playing surfaces to helmet gadgets that record impacts in real time. In fact a high-tech helmet with these gadgets and other new impact-reducing features is supposed to be rolled out for the 2017 season. Only time will tell what inventors may come up with, but as with diagnostic research, the key word here is *time*.

A third branch relates to changes to the rules of the game. Some rule changes have already been instituted in the NFL. You can't ram your helmet into somebody else's chin strap. You can't bazooka yourself into a defenseless receiver. These were skills that were actively coached back in my day; and back then, no player wanted to take abuse in a post-game film review for turning down a hit. Now it's different. But dialing back violence is a tricky business because, let's face it, violence is central to the popularity of the game. No one wants to watch flag football. Nevertheless, at some point, when the violence becomes egregious and gratuitous, it has to be restricted.

A fourth branch is treatment, or at least compensation, for victims. Treatment may be a ways off, until the research advances a little further along. However I personally have been involved in holistic treatment for almost a decade with Drs. Rick Sponaugle and Todd Pesek, and I have had positive results. So I do see some light at the end of the tunnel.

But compensation is an issue that can and should be addressed right now. For the record the NFL is currently taking steps in all these directions. In addition to the rule changes already mentioned, the League donated $1 million in 2010 to Boston University, academic home of Dr. Ann McKee, one of the early whistle-blowers regarding a possible link between football and CTE. Also, from what I have heard, the League has donated millions more since. The League has also invested millions in trying to develop some of the new technologies I referred to. Finally, it has agreed to pay out over $1 billion in a settlement with former players suffering from a range of concussion-related disabilities.

Let me be clear: I am not an apologist for the NFL. Lord knows, it took them long enough to face up to the problem; and whether the billion-dollar settlement is adequate is still an open question, in my mind. At some point the League has to answer the old Watergate questions of "what did they know and when did they know it?" In my day we commonly engaged in a farce, understood and accepted by players and coaches alike. When someone got his bell rung (read 'concussed') and couldn't remember his last name or what day it was, a coach, trainer, or doctor would hold up two fingers and ask, "How many fingers do you see?" The players always knew to answer, "Two." It was always two, never one, because that was too easy, and never three or four, because that was too hard. Always two, no matter what, and everybody knew it. So everybody passed the test and was cleared to go back in.

That was League-wide. Does the League have some culpability for deliberately ignoring a potentially serious problem? Lawyers tell me that beyond simple negligence, there is a buffet of doctrines ranging from gross negligence to recklessness to willful misconduct that could be explored.

But that said, fairness requires me to say that some steps are being taken, finally, and some compensation is being doled out. The League is not yet officially admitting any liability, but they are now certainly scrambling to come up with solutions. Attention is being paid.

Concerning legal liability, here's something to ponder: Suppose the NFL instituted a new contract provision that said something like, "Playing in the NFL carries an X% risk of CTE and may chop 20 years off your life." If they did that (and I promise you, it's coming), at least they could not be accused of concealing the risk.

There will be your Chris Borlands[23] who won't sign that deal. But I guarantee you there will be a whole lot of other guys who will. They will say to themselves, "I might – might – die at 55. In the meantime, I will be a multimillionaire, I will take care of my family financially, forever. I will be a hometown hero – maybe a national hero, maybe even a legend – and I will get to play the game I love at the pinnacle of my profession. Give all that

---

23 Chris Borland was drafted in 2014 by the San Francisco 49ers, but after a stellar rookie season, he retired in 2015, citing concerns over head trauma, not only his own, but the trauma he might inflict on opponents. As a result of his decision, he was obligated to return the lion's share of his $617,436 signing bonus and forgo future salaries in excess of $2 million per year.

up in exchange for the possibility – the *possibility* – that I might not live long enough to go through what Grandpa has been suffering for the last 20 years? Where do I sign?"

In my own, non-scientific survey on this question, how people respond depends a lot on their age. Older folks tend to pick the extra 20 years, partly (I think) because they are already running out of time, and partly because the fame-fortune-fun train left the station a long time ago for these people. Younger people tend to pick the fame-fortune-fun option for just the opposite reasons. Fame, fortune, and fun are primary goals at their early stage in life. At the same time old age is a distant and not very appealing prospect for them.

The real question here is not whether this is a good decision or not. Instead, it is who gets to make the decision in the first place. Should we have the government (or some other higher power, like the insurance industry or the plaintiffs' bar) make a blanket decision to ban football, or should we leave it up to individuals? It's a free country, right?

I seriously doubt that the government will outlaw football. It's too popular. Like I said before, we don't ban cars because of car accidents. We pass seat belt laws and we invent airbags and we crack down on drunk driving. But at the end of the day, we don't outlaw cars and make everybody ride the bus. Cars are simply too popular.

I'm more worried about the lawsuits, and I don't mean just the suits against the NFL. I'm talking about parents suing schools or community programs over youth football injuries, which could be a much more target-rich environment for plaintiff's attorneys. This is how we effectively banned smoking from public places. The first lawsuits seemed futile; but eventually the ongoing stream of lawsuits chipped away at the invulnerability of the tobacco companies. The issue gradually seeped into the public consciousness to the point that non-smokers acquired the courage to protest smoking in airplanes and restaurants and stadiums and other public venues. By the time the government got around to passing smoking bans, smoking in public was already a social taboo, thanks to the accumulation of who-knows-how-many private actions of protest.

Therefore, it is the private actions that I worry about most – the Will Smiths of the world pulling their kids out of the game because of risks that are still inadequately understood. I say *worry* because, at some point, if you pull enough kids out of football, you shrink the talent pool. If you shrink the talent pool, then at some point, the quality of the game deteriorates. If the quality of the game deteriorates, then sooner or later, people stop paying to see it, and it dies.

Why does that matter? Well, for one thing, football is a not insignificant part of our economy. I'm not just talking about the riches of the billionaire owners and the millionaire players. In addition to big businesses that profit from football, a whole lot of ordinary folks earn at least part of their living from football-dependent jobs, ranging from stadium employees to sports bar waitresses to the souvenir vendors outside the stadium. That's a lot of people to throw out of work in 31 cities around the country.

Also, think about the economics of our higher education system, specifically the athletic programs. Football and basketball pay the bills for a lot of other athletic and even academic programs. If you have a daughter in college who plays softball or runs track or rows crew, you should be a supporter of football since that's what subsidizes a good part of your daughter's coaches and gear and team travel expenses. If you ask any public university president what would be the impact on alumni donations of cancelling the football program, I suspect he would say something like, "Not much, actually – since I would be fired on the spot, and the program would be reinstated the next day."

Football also affects education in non-economic ways. At the high school and middle school levels, football is often the factor that makes participants pay attention to academics. If you don't keep up your GPA, you're off the team. Keep in mind that most football players do not come from privileged families, and very few NFL players come out of the Ivy League. Most (like me) come from working-class families (or poorer), where economic necessity tends to push education to the side in favor of early employment, often at some low skill, low-paying job. For many, many of these guys, football is the difference between graduating from high school, or not, or going to college, or not. It certainly was in my case. Without football there would have been no scholarship to Miami, and therefore, no Miami.

But I have a more personal reason for worrying about the future of football. Even though I myself may be Exhibit A in the case against concussions, I still believe that, on balance, football offers lessons you can't learn anywhere else. Odd as it may sound, I believe that in my case, even the brutality of the game was beneficial.

That statement may make you wonder if all my years in the game really did loosen some screws. After all the concussions, all the surgeries, the broken bones, the busted teeth, the torn muscles and ligaments and tendons, I still think brutality is a good thing?

Yes I do, and here's why. Every time I got knocked on my ass, or broke something, or tore something, or got my bell rung, or all of the above, the code of football required me to get myself up off the ground and get back to the huddle. I didn't even think about it. We still had work to do. My physical pain was irrelevant. The real pain, the pain that seared the soul, was the pain of losing. I would do anything to avoid that pain. In other words, I learned how to take a beating and recover. I learned to be resilient – a skill I certainly needed later in life.

You now know many of the ordeals I have gone through in my life. After each one, I have managed to pull my ass up off the ground and recover. I don't think of this as some kind of special feat. I think of it as a reflex I developed as a football player. Pain is irrelevant. I still have work to do. I am not going to lose in the Game of Life.

No other team sport can produce that kind of resilience, simply because no other team sport is as brutal as football. I pass over individual sports like boxing and karate, only because I have no experience in them. As team sports go, rugby may seem close to football, but without the pads, you can't hit anywhere near as hard as a fully armored football player. You can argue that hockey collisions are more violent because the players are moving faster, but hockey isn't designed for players to smash into each other on every play. You can argue that the NBA is the NFL without pads, but once again, the violence is intermittent. Nothing tops football for continual, full force impact.

The corollary, of course, is a whole lot of injuries, probably more than in any other sport. That is unfortunate, and as a parent myself, I understand the desire to protect children from pain and suffering. I could be accused of being over-indulgent with my kids in a number of respects. However, my son Joe plays football, even though I know that may mean more trips to the hospital, and definitely more trips to the trainer's room. I know better than most people because I lived it.

Does that make me a bad parent? Well, I did it myself when I was a kid. You might say that when I played, I didn't know any better. I was a kid, I thought I was invincible, and I was stupid. OK, all true. But if you asked me today if I would do it all over again, knowing what I know now about the pain, the physical disabilities, and, yes, some mental issues (like killer headaches and insomnia), my answer would be one word: Abso-freakin-lutely. I'd do it all over again in a heartbeat.

Part of my passion is an undying love of the game and the competition. Naturally I prefer the mental competition over the physical; but you can't have one without the other. It is the physical duress that makes the mental competition so challenging. How much more challenging would the game of chess be if 300-pound homicidal monsters were chasing you around while you plotted your next move?

But part of my love for the game has to do with the character-building. You get knocked down, you get back up, no matter what. I wouldn't have written this book – I couldn't have written this book – if I hadn't learned that lesson from all the punishment I took in football.

So, moms and dads, before you yank your kids off the football team, ask yourself this question: How well do you want them to be prepared to withstand the hardships that life is going to throw at them? Do you want them to have the fortitude to pick themselves up, no matter what, and move forward? If you do – if you value resilience – let them play.

Chapter 19
TRUTH

Attorney friends of mine tell me that one of the things you learn in law school is that there are many ways to tell the truth. That always sounded sketchy to me. But I suppose if your job is to present your client's case in the best possible light, and the job of sorting out the truth lands on the judge and jury, then being selective with the facts is sort of understandable.

I always preferred an expression I learned from a friend of mine who went through drug rehab: rigorous honesty. In rehab, Step One is overcoming denial. You have to be rigorously honest with yourself (and with others) about your situation, and admit the truth, the whole truth, and nothing but the truth – even if it makes you look bad. You can't fix a problem if you deny it exists. Rigorous honesty also requires you to apply the same candor to others. They can't overcome their problems if they are in denial. So you have an obligation to call them out when you think they are fudging facts or flat-out lying.

In my life in general, I have always tried to live up to the standards of rigorous honesty. At times it has gotten me in trouble. My career as a TV commentator for the Cleveland Browns probably would have lasted a lot longer if I had tapped the brakes a little on the rigorous honesty. Maybe if I had said things like, "I'm not sure that was the pass he wanted to throw in that situation," instead of "What the heck was he thinking? His X guy was wide open!" I might still be at the microphone.

But as a player, rigorous honesty always served me well. Problems in football could lead to serious injury, not to mention losses, and had to be addressed forthrightly and on the spot. Beating around the bush wasn't going to stop blitzing linebackers. I always found that rigorous honesty, often peppered with profanity to reinforce the effect, worked much better. And so with this book, I have tried to present my life and my thoughts with rigorous honesty. I have no doubt overstepped the bounds of good manners in some cases. I'm sure I'll get considerable blowback from my family. I hope they understand that I'm not trying to settle any scores. I hold no grudges.

And I hope I haven't blackballed myself out of the NFL with my views on topics such as concussions, the impact of big money, as well as my opinions on how to win. But I don't know how else to tell the story and still explain my views along with some of the unusual twists in my life that formed them.

At the same time I recognize that we all live in a universe in which the Earth seems to be the center, with the sun, the moon, and the stars all rotating around it. If you're standing in an open field looking up at the night sky, it seems like this is a reality. All the stars in the heavens seem to be shining directly on you. You forget that each star is actually shining outward, 360° in every direction, and not just on you. From your point of view, it seems like you alone must be the center of the universe. Of course the guy standing next to you is thinking exactly the same thing about himself.

The point here is that we all have our own perspective, myself included. I am not the All-Knowing, All-Seeing Eye of God. So as hard as I may try for rigorous honesty, I also recognize that there are many ways to tell the truth. So you have to be your own judge and jury regarding the explanations of things I have given you here.

In the very first chapter, I told you I had a couple success stories about the 'scrambling' mentality that I would save for the end. Well, here we are at the end, so here goes.

What I saved were two stories, one macro and one micro, to show you that there is life after loss, even if the loss is so brutal that you want to curl up in the fetal position and stay there.

The macro story is about my adopted hometown of Cleveland. As everyone knows Cleveland really took it on the chin, starting in the 1970's when foreign imports began to eat away at the dominance of American-made autos and the steel that built them – both on which Cleveland's economy depended. Factories closed and jobs were lost by the thousands upon thousands. Things got so bad that the city itself went into financial default in 1978. To add insult to injury, two Cleveland-born writers for the TV comedy show *Laugh-In* made the town into a national joke, literally. All the years that I was playing for the Browns, Cleveland was in the pits.

But Cleveland is a tough town. All that heavy industry in the boom years had attracted a lot of African Americans and blue collar ethnics – folks like my family – that gave Cleveland the personality of a working man's town: gritty, hard, nose-to-the-grindstone, resilient. These qualities are exactly what make Cleveland a great football city, even when the team stinks. Those crazies you see in the Dawg Pound on Sunday afternoons, with their dog masks and their orange-and-brown war paint, totally indifferent to whatever God-awful weather Lake Erie dumps on their heads – those people in many ways represent the heart and soul of Cleveland, as well as the Browns.

That heart and soul, that grit and resilience, that root-no-matter-what attitude, has brought Cleveland back from the dead. We still have work to do, but Cleveland has come a long, long way since I played in the 1980's and early 90's.

If you haven't been to Cleveland in a while, come take a look. Check out downtown, especially the food and entertainment scene on East 4th and West 6th streets. Maybe you and your family can have a picnic or take in a concert in the newly redesigned Public Square, in the heart of downtown.

Then explore some of the restored neighborhoods that feed downtown, like Ohio City and Tremont and Gordon Square, and Hingetown. Take a walk down to the Flats area by the river; it's not just a summertime playground anymore; new commercial complexes and apartments like East Bank are springing up. Then check out Playhouse Square, now reportedly the largest integrated performing arts center in the country after Lincoln Center in New York.

Leave yourself at least a few hours for the Rock and Roll Hall of Fame down by the lake next to the Browns' stadium. Then take a Health Corridor bus out to University Circle and check out the museums, and the Case Western Reserve University campus and Little Italy and Uptown. If you have aspirations to NFL management, continue up the hill a couple miles to John Carroll University, Don Shula's alma mater. You won't believe how many football execs have graduated from that place.

And if you're a health care worker, bring your resume. Cleveland Clinic and University Hospitals and MetroHealth are all booming. We may not make many car parts any more, but we can fix your body parts like no one else.

Other fun facts: the 'Cleveland Plan' for public education, which has the Cleveland Metropolitan School District joining forces with the city's top charter schools, is attracting nationwide attention. Also, did you know that Cleveland now has the highest per-capita density of Millennials with post-graduate degrees of any city in the country? It's true. The young people have figured out that you can live twice as well in Cleveland on $50,000 as you can on the coasts with $100,000.

So Cleveland is coming back, big time, and it's an exciting thing to watch and be a part of. I already mentioned that the Cleveland Cavaliers won the 2015-16 NBA Championship, at last driving a stake in the heart of the infamous 'Curse of Cleveland.' I myself got to ride in the victory parade, at the generous invitation of Cavs team owner Dan Gilbert, as did other Browns veterans, including, significantly, Earnest Byner. It was perhaps the happiest event in Cleveland since the end of World War II. Official estimates put the crowd at 1.3 million, which equates to every man, woman, and child in Cuyahoga County. People came from all over Northeast Ohio, and for that matter, a number of other states, to celebrate our civic emancipation from the Dark Age that Cleveland had suffered through.

But Cleveland's recovery would not have happened if everyone had just given up on their city and moved to Florida. No, it happened because a lot of Clevelanders refused to give in to the trials and tribulations of Rust Belt decline. Instead, they dug in and worked hard and put a lot of money at risk, and they made it happen. They scrambled and battled back.

The micro story I saved for last is about me. As you know by now, if you didn't before, my life after football has been no walk on the beach. Maybe I should apologize to all those who expected my book to be nothing but first person NFL highlights and hilarious locker room war stories. Instead, I have burdened you with financial catastrophes, family issues, personal problems, and the battle scars of uncountable football injuries. You were expecting a fountain of football, and instead, I gave you the Professor of Pain. But I had my reasons.

I wanted you to see all the grief that can happen, even to someone who seemed to 'have it all.' Are you feeling strapped for cash? Try Chapter 7 of the Bankruptcy Act. Are you wondering where the love has gone in your life? Go through a protracted divorce with a person who has BPD. Are you feeling insignificant? Consider the perils of celebrity (forget me – think LeBron). Frustrated by the aches and pains that accumulate with age? Break half the bones in your body and bang your head against a wall for 14 seasons.

I'm not trying to make you feel sorry for me. On the contrary, I'm trying to tell you I feel your pain, in spades. I've learned something about adversity over the years, both from football and from life in general. And I think I've learned something about how to deal with it.

In case you're wondering if I am now living in a homeless shelter after all my troubles, or eating out of dumpsters, the answer is no, I am not. For one thing, I have a great gig at the Rocksino in Northfield, Ohio, thanks to my good friends, Jim Allen and Brock Milstein. Jim is the Chairman of Hard Rock International, headquartered in Florida, and Clevelanders know Brock as the owner of the Rocksino, a gaming and entertainment destination midway between Cleveland and Akron that includes a horse race track, 2300 gaming machines, a Hard Rock Live concert hall, and a Kosar's Woodfire Grill. Jim and Brock had faith in me when I was at rock bottom (2009, the year of my bankruptcy), and brought me in as a partner in the steak house and a lot more.[24]

Also, in season, I am doing some talk radio and TV sports shows again, which I love, and media interest seems to be picking up. I still have my family farm in Ohio, thanks to some help from a savvy group of new business partners (guys I can actually trust), and I have my kids up there to goof around with me as often as possible. I'm doing better and better. I've even had some conversations with a few NFL organizations about

---

24 I mention Brock Milstein here in part because his relationship with his father Carl was as good as my relationship with my dad was bad. Carl Milstein was a major developer in Cleveland for many, many years, and his dying wish, almost literally, was to build a casino at Northfield. He didn't live to see it. But he had attentively groomed his son Brock in the business, and Brock was able to fulfill the dream on his father's behalf. It was a gratifying triumph to witness, and for me personally, they represent the gold standard in father/son relationships.

possible positions. Plus, every book I sell helps the comeback, so thank you very much for your support!

At the end of the day, I don't have the eight-digit net worth I once had, and I probably never will again. But I am paying the bills and working on a legacy for my kids. And the truth is, crazy as it may sound, I'm actually happier without all the millions. Big money can be like big fame. Be careful what you wish for. You may think that big money means a life of luxury. What you don't realize is that hordes of people will be clawing at you to get a piece, and that trying to appease them all can be an agonizing exercise in futility. Believe me, life is far more peaceful for me now without all that grief.

In sum, I'm ramping up instead of down. I have a future again, instead of a living hell. Like my beloved Cleveland, I have scrambled out of the pits, and I am moving forward. I'm as happy as I have been since those blissful early days in college when I was Bernie Who? I may have some lost yardage to make up, but I'm back in the game. Look out, World. Bernie Kosar still has some bombs to throw!

So what's the secret to life after loss? You can probably guess, from everything that you've read so far. In my mind, there's only one way to deal with adversity:

Learn to Scramble!

A WORD FROM THE SCRIBE

I always wonder when I read a book authored by some famous guy 'with' some non-famous guy: how much did the famous guy actually write? I will tell you right off the bat that this is Bernie Kosar's book through and through. It's not a transcript of Bernie monologues, obviously, but it's not far from it.

The stories are 100% Bernie's. Nobody could make up the incredible things he's been through, not only in football, but in the rest of his life. In many ways his business career after football is even more astounding than his gridiron accomplishments.

And the imagery used to tell his stories is pure Bernie. He comes up with expressions like "my blood pressure went to 2,000 over tilt" off the top of his head. I am confident he could have been a writer himself if he had chosen to go in that direction.

But most of all, the insights you encountered in each chapter come from his own unique perceptions, as refined by years of thoughtful reflection. Believe it or not, Bernie Kosar is a cerebral guy, with a lot of interesting views on a range of topics. And when he talked football, I was like a kindergartner in a graduate school course, desperately trying to keep up. If my fingerprints show up anywhere in this book, it is in the inadequacy of an ordinary fan trying to do justice to BK's football genius.

When I was first asked if I would help Bernie get his story down on paper, I thought it was a trick question. Of course I'll help. What proper Clevelander wouldn't give his eyeteeth for a chance like that?

The opportunity was even more enjoyable than I had anticipated. Bernie Kosar is the last thing you would expect as a celebrity. He is a self-deprecating, friendly, funny, warm-hearted regular guy. If you met him in a bar and didn't recognize him (assuming that were possible), you would think he was just one of the guys. Unless the conversation turned to something like the NFL draft, you would never know what an amazing life he has had.

The upshot is that I didn't just get to listen first hand to the exploits of one of my all-time, hometown heroes. I also got to make a friendship that I would never have expected in a million years. So I want to express my heartfelt gratitude to Bernie, for what I regard as an honor, on both counts.

Craig Stout

Craig Stout is a lifelong Clevelander who attended every Browns game he could afford when Bernie Kosar was quarterback. Now retired from a career as an insurance executive and technical writer, he remains active as CEO of the Arminius Foundation, which he founded in 2004, as a writer, and as principal owner of the Akron Racers (see footnote 4). A graduate of Williams College and The Ohio State University College of Law, he resides in Shaker Heights, Ohio.

red 90 zero T.O.
OPP puss 7 split T.O.
red 96 split T.O.
OPP 96 (86) HBSO split zid
jim 46 D T.O.
t pun 6 or 7, teven split T.O.
i bachu arrow

70 SSL
tem 92, 94 (alert H
70 (TS) Q curl out Q
70 flank hitch out Q
tem 92 bat HB ov

grn zone +10

ORANGE

TE cron
slot cron
7 im BOX
zero (CB)(T.o.)
, 66, 86

Dw
87 TE cron
67 slot cron
QK bat, 46

Squirm 96 QK,
flank rex FBAV
62 TE choice
74 (alert hit

Move orbit 96 HB arrow
deep 40, 62 deep m
move flank motion

GRN +20 BASE

tem 92, 94 alert HB late
MOVE zoom 62 FB arrow
2 FLANK rex FBAV HB inside
teven split Q HB inside
6 jim slot option HB inside
MOVE 62 deep m flanke
7 cherie (MOVE)
m-ORB.T 96 read HBS o
split zid

3RD DN 20 xyd 6
Sherel, 55 ser, Crul
86, 86 split let
66, 66 flank rex
84 Cherie
fly 92 (HB delay on
Split zoom 86 (99) OOL
BACK let 86 cru TE stem
fly 92 smash TE B.o. (out HB de
86 cyc (FB delay)
72 cu (TE stem)(FB delay